GW01548348

A Manual For Learning Blindfolded Sight & Chi Generation
The Fundamentals
Book 1

We can teach the blind to see. Let's change the world.

Author: Robert Smith

TABLE OF CONTENTS

Section 1
Dedication
Table of Contents:
Preface: How I got here
Chapter 1: Breath-work, Science & Chi
Chapter 2: Third Eye Secrets
The Third Eye Can Do More Than You Think
Chapter 3: How to Become an Enlightened Master
Chapter 4: How to Become an Immortal
Love, The Key to Live Forever
Chapter 5: The Secret to Manifestation
Everything is Spirit, Nothing is Matter
Chapter 6: Chakras & Enlightenment
Chapter 7: The Tree of Life
Chapter 8: The Real Purpose of Meditation
Chapter 9: Are Jedi Real? Yes, and so is The Force
Chapter 10: Kids and Blindfolded Sight
Chapter 11: Adults and Training Blindfolded Sight
Conclusion

A Manual For Learning Blindfolded Sight & Chi Generation
The Fundamentals
Book 1

We can teach the blind to see. Let's change the world.

Author: Robert Smith

DEDICATION

This book is dedicated to all life on earth and is intended to pre-serve hidden knowledge, and awaken a new generation to non-duality. This is for the seeker who wishes to go where others overlook. This is a hardcopy of the teachings I have learned and wish to pass on to the world. I honestly believe this can change the world. This will give you a step by step guide on how to learn Blindfolded Sight. As well as perform specific movements and breathing to awaken the energy inside you. You will learn to sense, manipulate, and build energy stores with proven methods. I will teach you everything I learn. This is only the beginning. We can teach the blind to see. Let's change the world.

PREFACE: HOW I GOT HERE

Hello, My name is Robert Smith, thank you so much for purchasing my book! I am so grateful! I am currently twenty-eight while writing this and what I've been discovering, I have to share it with the world! We are truly stepping boldly into the future, as this knowledge and the internet cover the planet.

In this introduction, I will tell you about how I got here, and how I came upon this sacred knowledge. What I have discovered, I truly believe can change the world, and it starts with changing yourself. I will share with you everything I have learned.

I am currently living in Washington Terrace, Utah. It's a beautiful place surrounded by red rocky mountains. Some of which I have hiked to find peace and solace. I was born in Fremont California in July, 1992. I have the zodiac sign of a cancer if you pay attention to that sort of thing. I am still on my hero's journey. I heard the calling, and I took action. This whole thing has truly left me in awe. Please, join me on this journey as I learn all I can and pass it on to the modern world. I feel like this knowledge and information has been hidden and kept secret for far too long. We can live in a magical future full of wonder and mystery. Life should be about discovering awe and being happy. There is so much that we are unaware of and still rediscovering.

My journey started a few months ago in March of 2020. I used to be open as a child, then I grew to be skeptical of everything. As I got older I began looking into quantum physics, and gained a

new perspective to help me navigate the reality before me. I discovered the dual slit experiment, which showed that electrons fired through two slits acted like waves when no one was looking and acted like particles when there was an observer. So with that, I learned that just by being here, just by observing, you are changing reality. How much power do we have to shift reality? What are our manifestation capabilities? Quantum physics opened my eyes once again to the infinite possibilities of the cosmos and this wonderful world we live in. Quantum physics gave me back power in my life. I used to feel like things happened to me, and now I feel like I happen to things.

Some other amazing experiments and breakthroughs show us that we can shift the outcome of a random number generator with our thoughts. If the generator only spits out ones and zeros, we can change the 50/50 distribution of numbers to one side or the other solely with our intention. This was also interestingly displayed by several random number generators around the United States that all started spitting out the same numbers, showing some kind of effect from the global consciousness field. We have the ability to affect random generators on a massive scale as a collective. Many devices have been created using biofeedback utilizing these phenomena. One, for example, is a light that will change to the color you are thinking of, when you put your intention on the lamp itself. I do also want to mention a few more experiments regarding random number generators. There is one with a light that randomly circles a room. However, when a plant is introduced into a corner of the room, the intention of the plan affects the random number generator, and makes the lamp shine more often in the corner that the plant is in. This same thing was demonstrated in another experiment using a robot that randomly walks around a room. When baby chicks were introduced, they imprinted on the robot and began following it around the room. They then removed the chicks, and put them in a cage on one side of the room. The chicks were able to shift the robot's random walking around the room, to stay on the half of the room the chicks were on. We affect reality. And our brains are the control

7

panel.

I heard from a quantum physicist on a Netflix documentary propose an interesting theory. He gave the analogy of a passenger on a plane, while it barrels down to crash. Now, if you are that person, you may feel like there is no way any of this could be your fault, or your doing. After all you are a passenger, and not the pilot. How could this be your manifestation? This physicist's idea is so radical, it is hard to believe. However, this is what new-age science is pointing to. Quantum physics is the marrying of science and spirituality. You are an infinite being capable of manifesting any future you desire. This gave me hope. I'm not a victim, I'm a creator.

When you feel a happy emotion like joy, gratitude, compassion, or love for example, you produce a larger electromagnetic field around your body, originating from your heart. You also produce chemicals that activate new protein production and can even affect and change gene expression. The same goes for negative emotions as well, and stress hormones. Your body can get addicted to a specific kind of emotion and chemical make-up. You will re-live scripts from previous instances. We get caught in a routine and don't often adventure out from the patterns we are used to. This is due to survival and how our brain tends to wire. Here, we have to realize we are not the brain, which is part of the body, and conditions us for habits. This is also where the subject of ego can be discussed. Your ego is like a little monkey on your shoulder telling you what you have already heard and building subconscious patterns we can feel stuck in. You are not your ego. To transcend, you must get past the ego. I have a wonderful meditation I was going to roll out, and I just received confirmation, from further research, that I am absolutely on the right path. It's all about love and compassion. It's incredible the physical changes it makes. I've always had the knowledge that all is one, but it took a while to connect the dots, and be able to explain how that could truly be.

In March of 2020 Coved-19 started to become a bigger deal than we were lead to believe. The company I was working for went

bankrupt, so fortunately I was able to go on unemployment. Staying at home all day, I got pretty bored with Netflix and TV. I started just doing educational research and trying to learn more about aliens, our history, and everything not taught in school. Speaking of aliens, I have seen a few UFOs in my life, or at least that's what I believe them to be.

I was camping as a child with my family and up near Clear Lake, California. It was a late night and the stars were bright. There wasn't very much light pollution, so we would go down to the lake, and listen to old Native American tales of things like, why the turtle has a shell. They were often something like that. One night I was down by the cabin, and I looked up at the stars. Two of them seemed to be moving. They took several right turns and disappeared. Then they reappeared, and continued zooming around in the sky, going left, right, up, and down. I saw my step sister and had her confirm I was seeing, was actually what I was seeing. They flew around for about five minutes, then disappeared.

We can't be the only beings in the universe. The math doesn't play out that way. I believe someone said that there are as many inhabitable planets as grains of sand on the earth. I had to learn more. There are always great documentaries out there, and one person I found, that I knew was credible, was Dr. Steven Greer. I absorbed as much of his work and material as I could. After the CE-5 documentary came out, I was introduced to the idea of remote viewing.

CE-5 stands for, human-initiated contact or contact of the fifth kind. Steven Greer has been doing this for the past 30 years and has hundreds of recorded UFO sightings. He has compiled over 400 highly official, credible members of the military and many other secret groups. I knew he was legitimate and I had to learn as much as I could. I may as well share the process and method for a successful CE-5 contact here. First, you will need several people to join you at a remote location that is very dark. You don't want any more than 12 people, as it becomes more challenging to find heart and mind coherence throughout the group. You will want to circle up and begin doing a 30-minute meditation, basking in

radiant joy, and feeling your body vibrate. let go of all senses and let your focus widen. By letting go with radiant joy you create a much larger electromagnetic field around your body and connect with source energy. After finding heart coherence after maybe 5-10 minutes then you will begin vectoring in any spacecraft that may want to pay a visit. The process begins by imagining the space above you, and your perspective is that of a bird looking down. Slowly you zoom out, with great visualization, until you see the group, the surroundings, and the clouds. Eventually, you will zoom out and see the whole earth, the milky way, and out beyond into the cosmos. With a friendly, non-violent intention, you can politely invite anyone to come and say hello. You now reverse the zooming process and begin zooming down into the outer arm of the milky way and toward the sun and the earth. You will go all the way down into your continent, into your state or location, and down to your group. This process is repeated up and down to show your location in the cosmos and your intent. This was my first introduction to remote viewing. According to Steven Greer, the way that interstellar civilizations communicate is through consciousness. The speed of light is not fast enough to convey information across space in a timely manner. So instead we have a quanta of thought. Also remember, all points in space and time are one. I also got this saying from one of the gentlemen that Steven Greer interviewed. Watch his stuff, and pay attention. The future is going to be wild and wonderful, and it's up to us to make it a reality sooner rather than later.

Dr. Steven Greer introduced me to the Vedic Scriptures and the siddhis they mention. These superpowers, were written about in ancient India in Shambhala times. This also introduced me to Sanskrit, which is referred to as the language of consciousness. Many old Buddhist texts were written in Sanskrit and there are several variations to the language itself. Today however it is a dead language and translations of texts can often have up to ten different interpretations. In these texts from thousands of years ago I found remote viewing was mentioned, among many other abilities. I will have more books teaching other abilities, but in

this book, we will focus on Blindfolded Sight, energy work, and connecting with the infinite.

I found that the CIA also had a psychic intelligence-gathering unit for twenty years. They spent millions on the project and had incredible success. I did further research on who was in the program and learned what I could about Russel Targg and Pat Price. I found Ingo Swann as well. So much compelling information only sparking my interest in this internal vision. It is possible, they couldn't have been making it all up with the coherence in stories and cultures around the world.

One day I stumbled upon an app that Russel Targg made called, "ESP Trainer". In this simple game, you must choose what the right color will be, out of 4 possible colors, to get the right answer. You must look into the future to see which of the four colors, red, blue, green, or yellow, will give you a point. There are twenty-four rounds, and on my third time playing the game, I received a 12/24 correct, when statistical random would be 6/24. I felt wonderful, I knew psychic phenomena had to be possible. I struggled to try and do some math for a few minutes to see what the odds are. Then I just resolved to creating a few charts and tracking my progress with each score recorded, at the end of every game for a few days. I felt my results were noteworthy. They had statistical relevance, but no one else believed that they could be anything more than chance.

I checked out Russel Targg's website and found that at one point, he and his team trained 145 NASA scientists in remote viewing. Within 1 year, 4 of them had reached the 99%+ accuracy range. This is incredible. I eventually started finding other schools around the world that teach this very same thing, or really something more advanced.

The main two that stood out were InfoVision by Mark Komissarov, and Vibravision coined by the Zeleznick Brothers, which utilized a technique they were fortunate enough to be the first foreigners to learn, from the royal family, in Java Indonesia. This is Merpati Putih, translated as the white dove. This system was passed down as the royal family's inheritance to the kings and

queens of Indonesia. In the 60's they released the system to the public because of the ability to give sight back to the blind. Thousands have regained their sight in Indonesia since then, and only in the year 2000 did the system make its way to America.

With Mark Komissarov's method, you use intuition as the main driving factor in the process. You must listen to the answers that come to you when you intend to know something. You must not guess. As time progresses you're able to recognize multiple objects in your field and the vision fills out from there. Mark does mention that people who are blind from birth take a longer time to develop sight, as they do not have a template for what things should look like. The time it takes should never deter you from what the end goal is. In reality, if you put in the time and train every day, you can learn very quickly. Faster even, than picking up a new job.

Mike and Nate Zeleznick, utilizing the MP method, approach blindfolded sight from a different angle than Mark. With M.P., you first start by sensing your own energy, and learning to manipulate it, and grow it. You must charge and build your energy banks with daily practice. In a way, when they see, it is almost like a radar. The practitioner sends out energy with their hand and feels what energy comes back. They are able then to slowly map out their surroundings with two main energy sensors. Their hands, as a flashlight, and their heart, used as a lantern.

All of this was so amazing! People in Indonesia are driving cars and motorcycles with their eyes taped shut. Blindfolded sharpshooters are shooting at balloons held by other people. They use their inner energy to assist in breaking things with their hands. I have also seen the use of telekinesis and other amazing abilities that come with this training.

On Father's day after a month or two of non-stop research, I created the website blindfoldedsight.com. If what I learned was real I have to learn and teach this. After all, kids can pick it up in thirty minutes! I felt so much joy and exuberance. Life just became so much bigger and brighter. I could hear the calling. This is my path. Using all my findings I started creating Online lessons to

help others achieve what I had discovered. I didn't quite have anyone to help me train consistently so I tried to be that for others through the internet. I then started planning for a move to Utah to learn Merpati Putih. I found a wonderful family with six kids! Well, I thought, this could be perfect. I can validate my findings and teach the kids impossible things. So I packed up, and I made the move!

The kids were a bit much at first, but as long as I'm able to get my alone time, I'm all right. I resolved to lots of hiking where I made more videos about the subject and some of the things I had discovered. I guess I'm going to be a Youtuber now, who could have guessed that? Eventually, the time came when I started teaching the kids. They progressed incredibly fast. I probably only worked with them for thirty minutes every other day. I did notice on the 4th day of practice, which was about 3 days after the others, the kid's skills had noticeably diminished. However after a little work, one of them, through perseverance, began doing well, really well. Maybe too well. I am hesitant to put up the 4th day of training on youtube as I'm not sure if there is any cheating involved. What I have learned from this experience is that the Mindfold mask is far superior to the other mask I got because I thought it looked "cooler". This second mask does let light in, and in the right positioning, does allow the wearer to see a sliver at the bottom of the mask. I have also heard from someone who took the course in Germany with Evelin, that having the masks a little loose may help people learn the skill. It may give their brain an excuse on how it may be possible and therefore allow it to start happening.

So several months have passed since I moved away from the kids. I have begun extensive research and found some remarkable things relating to blindfolded sight and enlightenment. This is only the beginning of an incredible journey. In the following chapters, I will go over the reasons for training blindfolded sight, as well as the end goal. I will be going over science and breathwork as well as chakras and understanding energy. We will explore our greatest potential and help usher in the brightest future possible.

CHAPTER 1: BREATH-WORK, SCIENCE & CHI

Why do Breath-Work?

Breath-work is a vital tool in energy generation through ATP (for all our energy uses).

The proper use of breath-work changes the user's physiology making it more oxygen efficient and allows the user to Increase red blood cell size and production.

Athletes find higher performance when training with intermittent hypoxia as first discovered via the high altitude of the 1968 Olympics in Mexico.

You create antioxidants battling the effects of aging.

You alkalize the blood removing acid from the muscles and stress from the body.

You help in water generation, some going to the thyroid helping it keep balance.

You improve your bone mineral density.

You improve your tolerance to CO_2.

You can also lower the CO_2 levels in the frontal cortex to change the chemistry and shut down the ego temporarily.

Hyperventilation Breath-work can bring about hallucinations by generating DMT.

Intermittent hypoxia breath work improves oxygen efficiency, antioxidant production, and cell longevity.

You improve the strength of your heart muscles and your cardio-vascular and nervous systems.

You improve your chi energy stores and widen your energy channels.

How?

Fast breathing, or hyperventilation, loads oxygen up on red blood cells, and because of the drop in CO_2 levels, they hold on to more oxygen than they release into the muscles. The blood alkalizes and the chemistry of the frontal cortex changes which can shut the ego off.

You find brain coherence and you balance the autonomic nervous system. This also creates oxidants and free radicals. Our mitochondria in our cells are about 98% efficient at turning oxygen into ATP. That remaining 2% of residuals can end up doing us harm.

Holding your breath through intermittent hypoxia does a small amount of stress to the system ramping up the production of antioxidants to deal with those oxidants, which can lead to aging in the body. Through holding our breath we strengthen the cardiovascular and nervous systems. You improve bone mineral density and start creating up to 10x more red blood cells. What seems like a form of adaptation, the body's red blood cells also increase in size and carrying capacity. CO_2 tolerance is then increased, which allows us to improve the efficiency of our energy generation from oxygen.

When we do slow breathing, it improves our lung capacity and oxygen efficiency. More oxygen is pushed into the muscles than before as an increase in CO_2 levels in the blood force the red blood cells to release the oxygen.

To begin improving function in the body a goal recognized in the Nei Kung practice is slow breathing, 15 seconds in 15 seconds out. You then move up to 30 seconds in 30 seconds out. It's said that a breakthrough happens at 1 minute in and 1 minute out. This is called turtle breathing, and further progress can still be made by increasing your time even more.

Exercise in the system, beyond the available oxygen in the muscles, begins ramping up ATP need and energy generation cap-

abilities. With the glucose and oxygen we take in from the environment we create ATP molecules which link 3 negatively charged phosphates together. They desperately want to separate, and when we use our ATP (energy stores), we shoot off a phosphate molecule breaking a bond and releasing free energy in a variety of potential forms.

ATP has stored energy that can be released when we call upon it through breaking down collected bonds like releasing a compressed spring full of kinetic energy. This energy can be released in any form of energy, such as electric, thermal, luminous, gravitational, electromagnetic, RF, and more.

How Long Do I do Breath Work?

It is reported that with 3 months of specific daily breath work, slow dynamic movements, breath retention, muscle contraction, and meditation creates significant physiological changes in the practitioner's body. This allows for improved strength, energy projection, brainwave control, electric field strength, and various other abilities that would be described as magic, such as telekinesis. It's measured that after chi practitioners perform their abilities their levels of ATP significantly drop.

One example of breathwork is this 6 reps of breath holds twice a day. I go over proper training methods in my blindfolded sight courses on my website blindfoldedsight.com. Please check out my 5-day workshop. Another great example is Wim Hof's breathwork method. 16,400 people volunteered to get injected with e-coli, and Wim Hof, with his breathing technique, was the only one to overcame the bacteria with ease. We also see with divers who did breath-holding, had 5% higher levels of hemoglobin in their blood, which means higher oxygen carrying capacity, and better performance. When you hold your breath, this triggers the mammalian die response, which then activates the vagus nerve, and lights up a connection between your brain and your heart.

Chi and Reality

Chi is a fundamental building block of all matter and the base

structure of all the elements. Chi is the psychic realm and the Akashic records. It is not bound by space or time. This is why you can do telekinesis over zoom. It is the zero-point energy field capable of providing us with unlimited energy, light, heat, and even transportation. The world will change once we learn to harness this field. Teleportation through these fields is possible and done today. All points in space and time are one. This is why remote viewing is possible. There is only one mind. All is one, and all is energy. Even at the most fundamental levels of matter, nothing is solid. Protons and electrons are just dense energy fields. To understand how psychic phenomena are possible you must first understand this. Second, you should know that information is energy, and third, the world operates on love. And only by working together can things exist. This is the universal law, act in love and you act in harmony with all. Anything else will slowly deteriorate until it is no more.

Conclusion

Do breathwork for energy generation, health, longevity, balance, stress relief, and more. Breath longer and slower throughout your daily life. Check out my workshop on my website where I teach you all I know, so you can learn to see without your eyes, improve your intuition, learn energy detection, generation and manipulation. To get the best results, it takes about 3 months of intro training and storing energy to be able to start excelling down the line. This is due mostly to the physiological changes we need to make. The younger you are, the less work you need to do to optimize your system for chi work. Don't do while driving or in water in case you pass out. Also, if you have any medical conditions, check with your doctor before doing any breathwork.

CHAPTER 2: THIRD EYE SECRETS

The Third Eye Can Do More Than You Think

Many people understand that your third eye is your intuition, but most people in the west are unaware of its true potential. When you hear someone say that their third eye is open, there is a very good chance that it is not quite as developed as they may believe. I would be willing to bet that a majority of psychics and tarot card readers are no more psychic than the average person. Now don't get me wrong everything is possible, but the reality for most psychics is if I were to blindfold them and ask them what color I have just handed them, with a 25% chance of getting it right, the majority wouldn't fair better than a 31% accuracy rating.

We all know your third eye is a thing, after all the CIA spent millions of dollars on the "Stargate Project" from 1978-1991 at Fort Meade in Maryland. A majority of us are also aware that there is a military-industrial complex with a black budget that works on UFOs. Thanks to Steven Greer, who has put together extensive stores of information on these subjects from over 400 current and retired high-level military officers who have come forward with documents and proof. So it's no wonder that the Stargate program was shut down in 1991 when things were just starting to get good as far as discovery goes. It was time to go off the books. A few of

their findings were made public due to the freedom of information act.

The CIA found that astral projection and, remote viewing were possible. They also studied kundalini theory and found some remarkable things. Remote viewing and astral projection are just the start. In this magical world we live in, these abilities can become even more refined and perfected. The Gateway program at the CIA was able to go in spirit to the kremlin, and see things like a hidden security area below Putin's desk. The Gateway program was developed by Robert Monroe as a practical means to learn and improve your ability to astral project. Robert Monroe even reported being able to poke someone, and they said they felt it, and they had a mark in the corresponding place following the encounter. Things like this are also reported in books such as the *Autobiography of a Yogi* and *The Life and Teachings of the Masters of the Far East*. Masters of astral projection in these books literally create a second body they can interact with others through. Amazing stuff. Many people would believe it's not real, but I can assure you, it is.

Remote viewing uses our third eye and our intuition to gather information. Our pineal gland also can produce colors in the darkness of our closed eyes. Just like when we are dreaming we can produce DMT to see colors and light. Some remote viewers in the Stargate program reported less seeing but more knowledge and feeling. A random thought would pop into their mind or a feeling. This like the astral projection is just the beginning. It gets much clearer with time. The problem I see with these experiments, is that they started at far too large of distances and far to complex images. Places are hard and there are so many subjective aspects. Yes, they are wonderful and proved that all points in space and time are one, but they should have started with much simpler training rather than jumping into the deep end.

How do You Open Your Third Eye?

When developing blindfolded sight we start with simple colors and a blindfold. The goal is to learn to pick up information in

front of you before you try and look across the world, with something hard to verify. You need to have biofeedback so you can better train your intuition. This is where another misconception about the third eye comes in. Your third eye is never really closed. So in contrast there is no real opening it. It is more like a muscle. If you train it then you can learn to trust it. Most of us have no idea what a true intuitive hunch feels like, let alone being able to get any real information from it. It is always there, but you have to learn what information is intuitive and what information is just your overactive imagination. To do this you need to train, and you may be wrong until you learn what the right answers feel like.

How Does our Intuition Work?

Well, everything is energy, even at the smallest levels, electrons and protons are just dense fields of energy. Nothing in our world is solid. Next, you must know that all information is energy as well. This ties in deeper into the fields of chi that permeate and surround us, and record everything that happens. This is what the Akashic records are, and when we can learn to decipher chi into the information that it carries we learn to access the Akashic records, and the storage base of all information.

What Is Your Third Eye Capable Of?

Well, once your brain has learned to decipher chi, you can learn to see blindfolded. This is like learning a language, for example, when you feel the energy of color, you likely won't be able to tell the difference between the different colors themselves. Each object is constantly radiating energy that describes that object. We just have to learn to decipher it, like a language. There are very interesting examples discovered by Mark Komissarov when developing his InfoVision methodology. He found, after teaching a blind student his infoVision method, which trains your intuition, that the student was able to read a newspaper headline that was not written in brail. This was amazing and it led to many other wonderful discoveries regarding your third eye. This particular student was astonished as well because he had never seen letters

and wouldn't have been able to read them if he wasn't blind. Mark Komissarov has been an amazing figure in this field of study, which has largely been kept secret all over the world. The Royal Family of Central Java, also released a comprehensive energy development system which allowed completely blind people to learn to see again, and even do things like ride a motorcycle. I have been greatly inspired by both of these systems as well as several others. The possibilities only become more vast from here.

Not only are you able to see and be an expert sharpshooter while completely blindfolded, but you can also look into the past and even the future. Mark Komissarov would do tests with his students where he would place an object on a table for one minute. He would then remove the object, hide it, and proceed to open a door bringing in a blindfolded student. He would then ask the student to look one minute into the past and tell him what object was on the table, and they were able to do so. He then asked where he placed the object, and they were able to go back, and watch the scene to see where and what Mark had done in the room before they entered. Now if you're thinking that's truly amazing, it gets better.

Once you can improve your skills enough you can begin doing things like accessing any information off of any storage device. Now similar to the brail to letter conversion that happened a person, adequately trained in blindfolded sight, can hold a DVD in their hand and watch the DVD in their mind. And, not just watch it, but go through the menu and access different things like extended features. This same phenomenon can also be performed with a book, reading it without ever opening it. I believe some of this was referenced in the movie *The Men Who Stare At Goats* which is based on true events regarding the CIA and their psychic research. It is also shows that yes, they were able to successfully kill a goat by staring at it, using their abilities. Another interesting thing is that you can not only read the information off of a computer blindfolded but it's said you can also write information on the computer without touching it. Amazing stuff and all of these things only open larger doors.

Psychic abilities are very real. They develop remarkably fast when we are between the ages of 6-12. Indigo children are just regular children. We all have these capabilities. We need to re-shape our teaching system to include intuition training at young ages. Some of Mark's students who took his training reported seeing the bubbles on the right side of his test lighting up on all the correct answers before he had even read the questions. We can all learn to access the akashic records to receive the correct answer to any question every time, it just takes the proper training and dedication. The only problem is the older we get, the harder it gets. Much of this comes from our belief systems. When we have an unconscious belief and it faces off with a conscious belief, the unconscious one will win every time. A reason children are so adept to this stuff, is that they run around in delta and theta brainwaves, without a well developed analytical mind getting in the way. I want to remind you everything is possible! You are capable of anything! Develop your third eye, for practical, actionable uses. I will teach you how to sense, grow, and project your energy which will help you sense your environment (lead to telekinesis) and grow your intuitive skills.

CHAPTER 3: HOW TO BECOME AN ENLIGHTENED MASTER

What is Enlightenment?

Enlightenment has been misinterpreted in the west for some time now, and the meaning seems to keep shifting. Enlightenment in Buddhism means that you know everything. Now the first question you might ask is, how can one person know everything? That doesn't even seem possible. Well, I can assure you that it is indeed very possible through the use of the akashic records. The akashic records are a record of everything that has happened. Anyone who has developed their blindfolded sight and intuition can access all information that is currently, or has already been, imprinted onto the ever pervading fields of chi. Enlightened masters can even project this for others to see and have them watch the past as if on a tv screen before them. Our brains can access and decipher information from these chi fields, receiving knowledge from energy. Chi is an interesting phenomenon because it is not bound by time or space and can be both here and there. One important mechanism that allows all of this to take place is the fact that all points in space and time are one, and also

similarly that information is energy.

Once we can harness the chi fields we will be able to do some of the things enlightened masters can do. We will have access to an unlimited source of energy and heat. The chi field is the zero-point energy field and the akashic records so, once we gain control over them, technologically we will be able to look through time and watch past events unfold as they truly happened, on a tv screen. Many of these technologies have already been created and then suppressed. One device described by Dr. Steven Greer is a machine that deciphered white noise to be able to listen into the past at a given location. We have also seen this with several cameras that were created which could photograph the past. These things are real and have already been validated through modern technology Some of them are very likely taxpayer-funded and kept secret somewhere.

Children and Intuition

Now it's very well recognized that children have a far higher aptitude for acquiring and developing higher levels of intuition and energy manipulation. Part of this is because children ages 6-12 run around all day in delta and theta brainwave states making these kinds of things easier. This may also be due to adults having their pineal gland calcified from fluoride throughout their lives. All of these abilities are completely natural, so for children who haven't been taught otherwise they, come naturally. This is why so many people report having psychic children or indigo children. The reality is that everyone who is a human and who is conscious is psychic. Psychic abilities are more like muscles that you need to strengthen and not like gifts. So if all points in space and time are one, that also lines up with what many mystics around the world teach, which is, you are god. And if you are god, you are omnipresent, omnipotent, everlasting, and all-knowing.

Am I God?

Some of my favorite books are, *The Life and Teachings of the Masters of the Far East.* In these books, a group of American sci-

entists in 1894 goes over to India, Tibet, and the surrounding nations, looking for the masters they had read and heard about stories and books. These men ended up meeting many enlightened masters and traveling with them for several years. These scientists were utterly baffled when they saw men doing things like walking on water, manifesting food, levitating, teleporting, glowing, and much more. These masters were hundreds of years old and hardly ate, living primarily off of chi, or gods energy. They talked about how we are all one and how god is inside all of us. They taught that love is the universal law and anything that is not done in love will slowly fall apart over time. They taught that age comes from pain, misery, and anger, while youth comes from love, compassion, and selflessness. Now many of these things may be hard to believe but even one of the fathers of modern quantum physics Erwin Schrödinger said, "The total number of minds in the universe is one. In fact, consciousness is a singularity phasing within all beings."

In 1982, the Ark of the Covenant was discovered buried deep below where christ was crucified, 600 years before his crucifixion. Now, I'm not religious, but when they found the Ark there was dried blood on the mercy seat. In the bible, it says when Jesus was crucified, the earth shook. A crack had formed at the base of the cross where the blood drained down through the newly formed channel in the earth directly onto the ark of the covenant. There is a deeper story about what the ark is for and how the blood being on the seat may have been predetermined. However, I would like to talk about the actual blood analysis that was performed. This may shock you.

The Blood Analysis of Jesus. (Proof of Immortality)

When the blood was taken into a lab to be tested they started by rehydrating the blood over 72 hours with saline solution. After that time they found, with utter astonishment, that the blood was still alive. This is a first. Dried blood is known to be dead blood, however, after 2,000 years this blood was still alive. This allowed the scientists to perform further tests that would not

have been possible if the blood was dead and they found even more startling findings. The blood only had 23 chromosomes instead of 44 chromosomes which every other human on the planet has. 22 of those chromosomes were from the mother, which means that all of the traits of Jesus had to have come from his mother. And 1 chromosome was identified as coming from the father. The only problem was that the chromosome was labeled as, not originating from a human male.

Incredible, so with this one blood sample we see that not only immortality, and Jesus were real, but also the immaculate conception. Our world is a lot more magical than most of us think

Enlightened Masters are Real

There are people today that would be considered immortal. Many of them are referenced in the "Life and Teachings of the Masters of the Far East" books. The group of scientists ended up meeting Jesus, as a living, breathing, miracle performing, man on their journeys. He explained that he wishes that people will try to know him as he is and stop focusing on him as he was on the cross. He explained what he meant in his teachings, telling people that God is within them. He wanted to show man that he was capable of everything that Jesus himself was capable of. Unfortunately, people began worshiping him as a god and he did not want this. He saw the shift happening in the future and decided it was time to go. He didn't die though. He is alive today according to these books and the blood.

How do we Achieve Enlightenment for the World?

So my thought process is this, we need to add an ESP class in schools, because kids ages 6-12 learn blindfolded sight very naturally. By the time kids are age 12, 90% of them could be getting 100% on every test regardless of the material. If we train the next generation with their intuition and they can find the correct answer every time, then just imagine what we could accomplish. All of our problems will have clear paths to resolutions and we will begin living in Shambalah like times again. Everyone will see the

importance and validity of spirituality, done through practical means. People will be flying and teleporting. It will be amazing but we have to make it that way. If we don't, then technology may make spirituality silent, for god knows how long. It's up to us to be the change we want to see in the world. Blindfolded Sight will open so many doors, it's hard to truly imagine how great things actually can be. The implications of this all are extremely vast.

How do I Achieve Enlightenment?

If you are older, things like blindfolded sight are harder to learn, but that doesn't mean you should give up. Along with training your intuition becoming an enlightened master requires mastering all aspects of your existence. This means having emotional control and only acting in love. One thing we find when people start to rise in energy levels, the potential for harming yourself, or others, becomes very real. One must maintain emotional control or you risk serious injury to yourself or others. A few of John Chang's students ended up dying of organ failure, most likely due to these reasons. Not only must you master your emotions, because of how linked they are to your subtle bodies, but you must master your mind, and your body. You must change your physiology through breath work and meditation. You must master energy manipulation, telekinesis, pyrokinesis, levitation, and teleportation. You must master your mind and undo your programming. The biggest thing that holds us back from doing the impossible is our subconscious. If there is ever a battle between your subconscious and your conscious mind, your subconscious will always win. In Mo Pai Nei Kung there are 72 recognized levels a person must master to achieve Nirvana and become an Immortal Enlightened master. Many other practices have turned out Enlightened Masters aside from Mo Pai, I believe Merpati Putih has also allowed people in the past to achieve the highest attainment. The first step however is just mostly breath work and meditation to get the body energetically and physiologically capable.

CHAPTER 4: HOW TO BECOME AN IMMORTAL

Love, The Key to Live Forever

Love is the most powerful force in existence. This is how you can become immortal. Love is far more than an emotion, but rather, it is God. There are many laws, rules and karmic repercussions in this life, but when we act in love, we transcend those limits. When we act in love, we do the ultimate work. This extends into various other realms and levels of existence that most of us are unaware of. First, karma is real. When we take action it ripples out to the ends of the universe, touching all existence, then it returns to its source multiplied and amplified. Second, God is love. Only man does evil things, and yet, God is all things. So we are God as men, but when we do not act with him we lose his energetic support. We have free will. Our energetic body is the base of our physical body. Our consciousness comes before the brain, and is responsible for its formation. We must know everything is energy, and everything is one. Remember, "The total number of minds in the universe is one. In fact, consciousness is a singularity phasing within all beings." Erwin Schrödinger.

God has one law, and that is the law of love. Anything done, not following that law, will slowly disintegrate until it is no more. This includes our bodies and aging. Negative, painful, and fear-

ful thoughts create age, while loving, opulent, compassionate thoughts create youth. Love can make you younger. This isn't just a teaching of the Masters of the far east, but it is also represented in science in a few forms. For example mediations with higher vibration energies such as love and compassion, can affect your genetic expression, and increase immunoglobulin A levels by nearly 45%. This was demonstrated in some of Dr. Joe Dispenza's findings. This promotes fantastic healing. One thing Joe is still on the hunt for is activating the gene for immortality. We know we have it, because of cancer, but we haven't been able to properly utilize it. He also found through love, people were able to lengthen the telomeres at the end of their DNA strands, which promotes a longer life. In many ways, science has not caught up to the reality of our world and our existence. This is very evident through the knowledge that people out there are flying and teleporting without any current scientific understanding as to how.

There are Immortals Among Us

There are people out there who are hundreds and thousands of years old. They have been recorded throughout time, all over the world, even in our modern era. I recently watched David Verdesi talk about his experience meeting a man over 900 years old with records and evidence to prove it. David Verdesi is an interesting man in modern times who has traveled the world and trained with mystics in South America and Africa, saints in Russia, xian immortals in China, enlightened beings, as well as Tibetan and Buddhist monks. David himself is someone who has levitated before and accomplished superhuman abilities, or Siddhis. Through various references, I strongly believe that everything in "The Life and Teachings of the Masters of the Far East" is true. The internet is truly a remarkable thing. Soon I will be learning from individuals who have accomplished these things and again I find that love is a vital key.

The Key to Enlightenment

In the books by Baird T. Spalding, we learn from the masters that

there are many paths to attaining enlightenment and becoming immortal. One path is to train for many years, or potentially move away and live in a cave to devote countless hours to perfecting all of your inherited gifts. A second path is to learn to think and be only love. They say that only through love is a man truly free. The idea is that a person has unconditional love for everyone and everything. For everything is God, and God is love. This is also a fundamental trait of all enlightened masters, and it is a requirement to conquer death. Jesus is an enlightened master remember, and through this, he has also conquered death and walks the earth today.

Information is Energy

Every thought we have goes forth from us as a force with an energy of its own. When we think with words and directed attention that energy generally flows directly in a straight line, or sine wave, to the intended target. However when we think in pictures and emotions that thought goes out like waves from a drop in water, rippling out to all existence. These thoughts will always return to the sender with amplified force. Many people do not realize that we have immense power. We have all the power of God, as we are him and he is us. We just must abide by his rules or we will have to start over from the very beginning and try again. The only way to truly ascend is through love. Negative thoughts and intentions will only come back to us and keep us in a karmic loop of life and death.

Maintaining Your Subtle Body

Your subtle body is something that western science has not been able to grasp, but in China, these things have been known, and the sciences refined, for thousands of years. For example, acupuncture is directly related to our energetic channels and subtle bodies. But before needing treatment, we should first know how to maintain our subtle energetic body for health and mastery, which leads to the highest levels of attainment. Love again is the key. You must not let negative emotions and feelings infect

your energetic body as they will create holes in your aura when they re-enter and drain your life energy. To prevent this you must maintain peace and love in your heart. And you must have unconditional love for all. Our minds can be like wild elephants but once we master them we have immense power.

To have unconditional love for all you need to understand that in this world of karma, good and evil. God is perfection, just as much, as God is all existence. So in this way we see that all existence is perfection. And being perfect is neither good nor evil. This is a concept created with duality. This point is made by several philosophers like Friedrich Nietzsche in, *Beyond Good and Evil*. However, Nietzsche was an atheist for his adult life and believed god was dead. It personally took me a while to come around to the existence of God. I don't imagine him as a physical man, even though, he could be if he wished. God is all things and connects in ways that form the most incredible super conscious thing ever, which is aware of itself, and is always learning, growing and expanding. And the only way, we can truly grow, is through love.

Now, when I say that love is the most powerful force in existence, I do mean that. Not only is love responsible for all existence, but it is what binds it all together through sheer will alone. Love can also be a shield and the key to becoming truly immortal. Unfortunately, love also has a very destructive defensive power. This is referenced several times with examples in *The Life and Teachings of the Masters of the Far East* books. I'll leave that for you to learn about on your own. Those books are true accounts and real facts. I highly encourage you to read or listen to them and take the teachings to heart.

CHAPTER 5:
THE SECRET TO
MANIFESTATION

Everything is Spirit, Nothing is Matter

Everything of form has come into form through visualization. Out of the ether, or fields of chi, matter arises. We first proved that this was possible when we discovered the Higgs Boson particle. Matter can indeed come from energy alone. We see this also in quantum physics when particles vanish from one point and appear in another. Very similar effects are also found when the dual slit experiment is performed with various particles. We see that matter exists in two states, a waveform, and a particle form. We find that just the act of observation collapses the wave function into a particle. This is a fantastic demonstration of reality, our existence, and also the mechanism for manifestation.

We have another perfect example of manifestation when we take a look at the placebo effect. Statistically significant results are found when we just use a sugar pill in place of real medication. When a person truly believes that they have taken the correct medication, and that it will indeed heal them, then very likely they will be healed. The mind can not only heal illnesses even as severe as cancer, but can cause them as well. How we maintain our state of mind directly affects the world around us as much as it does ourselves. Just by observing we energetically interact

and have an effect on the world. When we believe that a placebo medication is an actual form of medication then it works. The key thing to notice here is that the patient who is taking the medication believes that he will be healed. He sees himself being healed, and having acquired the solution in his mind, and he has acknowledged that this is how things are in the outer world as well. The final step to manifestation would be to have emotion related to the image and outcome you know to be true, holding firm with faith. This placebo effect is directly linked again to our emotions and our subtle bodies. We have the manifestation capabilities of God, so we must not misuse them. It can be compared to having a genie in a bottle. Be careful what you wish for. The law of Attraction (and true manifestation) does not discriminate good from evil.

In the previous section on love, I mentioned how karma works and how thoughts leave our minds with an energy of their own. If we are not careful they will return and cause holes in our aura and leak our energy. I also mentioned how thoughts can travel in a line or a wave. This is similar to the dual slit experiment. When we think in words our thoughts travel in a particle-like fashion. But when we think with images and emotions our thoughts act like a wave and have a more resounding effect. This is the key to true manifestation. The act of simply repeating something in your mind is not necessarily going to work. You have to include emotion, a knowing, a strong visualization, and you must hold it for long enough. Then it will come to pass. This leads to being able to manifest physical objects out of the ether. This is the same method that God used to bring everything into existence. For a long time, he came up with existence in the thought of perfect creation, and through visualization in the realms of our mind he spoke the word, actualize, and existence came to be. He is, even now, still forming his perfect existence, with his will, and waiting for us all to accept it.

The enlightened masters demonstrate these things far beyond wishing for money or a date. These masters bring bread into existence and food straight from the hidden, or what some would

call the 4th dimension. We are capable of manifestation like this, and it should be our life's work to raise to the level of attainment where one gets all of his needs directly manifest out of the ether. You are capable of everything God is capable of.

Everything is spirit, nothing is matter. Your body comes from your subtle body and your brain comes from your consciousness. In China, it's very well understood that if you have a problem with your physical body it's because you have a problem with your energetic body. Negative emotions are more destructive than we are aware of. Thoughts have energy, and they can leave us, and ripple out, only to return with increased strength. 99.9% of matter is empty space. And what we think is actually solid, at the smallest levels, we only find dense energy fields with nothing truly physical.

The Power of "I AM"

The statement "I AM" Is the most powerful manifestation phrase there is. This statement was first brought to us by Jesus, however, there is evidence that this statement originated before him as well. Here are a few "I am" statements made by Jesus. "I am the resurrection and the life," "I am the light of the world," and "I am the door." This simple phrase, "I am the door," is telling us that the doorway to god can be opened with "I am" as "I am" represents God. The Masters say that long ago there was a time when man and god were truly one, in a world of non-duality. At this time, all was one, and harmony covered existence. Then man, being of God and from God, had the same manifestation power that God does. From this man began to create separation, until this existence was changed into a dual one. Man was then separated from who he truly is and he slowly lost his connection with the divine. Fortunately, there are Masters out there that still inhabit the earth. Some of them are the teachers of Jesus when he was a young man and traveled East. Several historic records follow his journey, however, most are not public. This is where Jesus learned to become an Enlightened Master likely studying Buddhism.

With "I am", Jesus was giving us instructions and guidance on

how to manifest. He was showing us that when we use the "I AM" statement we are acknowledging the God within us. There are several books on this topic and some of my favorites are the *I AM Discourses* by Guy Ballard (who claims he channeled St. Germain when writing the books). Guy Ballard is the founder of the "I AM" Activity and the St. Germain Foundation in the 1930s. In his books, he describes meeting St. Germain and learning the ways of the Ascended Masters. One of the most powerful tools that they use, many times a day, is the "I AM" Statement. He speaks about how these simple statements and a life of love are the keys to shaping the very reality you are surrounded in. I recommend listening to these books on audiobook, there are several on youtube. Every night when I go to bed I say to myself, "I am the embodiment of perfect health. I am eternally young in my spirit and my body. I am Perfection." These statements can also be used to help in shaping your own body or dealing with health problems. You just must be consistent and know it to be true.

This World is Real not a Simulation

Many people believe that we are in a simulation and that this existence is closer to the *Matrix* movies. This is not a simulation and you are not sitting somewhere asleep in a pod while a machine drains your life. This is all real, and is all spirit in constant expression. If we do not believe that and we think we will wake up when we die, unfortunately, that's not the truth. Our bodies will be turned to dust, and we will return to the eternal mind from which we came from outside of space and time. We will live in the energetic psychic realm of chi until we are reborn again.

Reincarnation Until we Get it Right

We do reincarnate, This is an interesting phenomenon proved time and time again all over the world. The Bible even used to have reincarnation in it until Constantine came along and nearly 42 books were lost when we were given a redacted version of the bible, leaving out certain keys and universal truths. The Dali Lama chooses the place and time that he will reincarnate and in-

forms those around him. Then at the given time they go to the village and bring a large number of toys to bring to children around the town, and when the right child chooses the right 3 toys and is able to identify a few key people, he is declared the Lama and his raised for greatness from that point forward. We've heard of children telling stories of dying in war and even remembering their previous names. Sometimes children have birthmarks similar to the wounds that would have been present at the death of their previous incarnation. We will continue to die until we learn to express love unconditionally for all and transcend death.

CHAPTER 6: CHAKRAS & ENLIGHTENMENT

Fifteen thousand years ago, Adiyogi (the First Yogi), which was Shiva, attained enlightenment and brought us all the Vedic science of yoga. This science lays out a roadmap that leads to the highest attainments. Yoga is far more than just stretching. One could argue that yoga is not about movement at all, but rather emotion and self-mastery. In the previous sections, we learned that our subtle body is where our physical body comes from. Like the question of the chicken and the egg, which came first? Consciousness or the brain? Consciousness came first and is responsible for the brain. We also learned previously that matter and spirit are not separate, but one and the same. Matter, is the expression of spirit, constantly unfolding in reality. Furthermore, we came across proof that immortality is real, and that the path to enlightenment is paved with love. This is clearly visible in the layout of the chakra system. You could describe this map to ascension as Jacobs ladder, a solid connection, or bridge, between the material and spiritual. I hope the picture is starting to become clearer. Everything is energy directed by intention, and every choice moves us closer or further away from the source of all. Chakras are the key to enlightenment in yoga.

Chakras are referred to as wheels, gates, whirlpools, or energy centers. They have acquired these names and understanding through the perception of the energy fields with refined sensing

and observation capabilities. When you have improved your own energetic senses and nervous system, you will sense these centers yourself. There are 114 chakras in and above the body, but most of the time we focus primarily on the predominant 7. These chakras, or gates, allow energy to flow into, or out of the body. This flow happens in the form of a whirlpool, spinning clockwise to condense energy into the body, and flowing counterclockwise when energy is leaving the body. Each of these centers interacts with the subtle world around us and affects us far more than most of us realize. In the East when there is a physical problem, traditionally they look for an energetic root cause. In the west, we are unaware of the impacts of subtle energies on our physical form and therefore disregard them entirely. Science, to our current understanding, backs the chakra systems. Each center, or system, is directly linked to a different set of organs that are responsible for specific actions in the body. This understanding of the energetic effects on the body, from emotion, is called biopsychology.

The chakras lay out a map of evolution starting at our root chakra, or Muladhara, moving from primal life in the physical world to our crown chakra, or Sahasrara, which represents God, and encompasses all existence both spiritual and material. The chakra system is for developing self-mastery, attaining enlightenment, and basically becoming a demigod. The science of yoga shows us that everything is connected. Everything is one, and the goal is to move from a duality based existence into a non-duality based existence. The goal of yoga is to raise your consciousness and understanding to that of God's level. The Vedic science of yoga allows us to see that in nearly every choice we make we are deciding between eternal life as perfection, or slow destruction clinging to selfish and materialistic ways. The biggest choices we make happen every day and determine our spiritual progress. Do you serve others, or do you serve yourself? This universe only works by working together, and if you serve only yourself you cannot possibly hope to ascend.

Each chakra is represented as a flower with a specific number of petals surrounding it. Each petal has a different meaning or trait.

The three chakras below the heart have petals that we would generally want to avoid. The petals surrounding the chakras above the heart are things we want to embody. These are called the vritti, or the propensities, of each chakra. The chakras below the heart represent our materialism while the chakras above the heart represent our divinity. Each chakra has a certain number of qualifications to truly open the gate and ascend to the next chakra climbing Jacob's ladder to meet God. This can also be related to the raising of the kundalini, but we will talk more about that later.

To get a base understanding of the chakras a good practice is to recognize where you feel certain emotions. This will help in understanding the chakras. When we worry it is felt in our gut and when we love it is felt in our heart. If you want a more visual image I suggest looking at the blood flow of the body in relation to different emotions. Our blood carries energy and it is moved depending on how we feel. Our emotions affect genetic expression and our physical health. Let's take a look at our chakra map, starting at the bottom, and the most material expressions we have, and moving to the top, at the most divine expression.

-Root Chakra – Muladhara (Red) I Am
Element: Earth
Symbolic Animal – Elephant

This center gives us a direct genetic link leading back to the first living organisms on earth. It is said that the genetic potential for immortality resides in this center.

The 4 petals or Vritti are as follows:

Kama ———————— This is the desire for material pleasure such as sex and food comes from our animalistic instincts.

Artha ——————— This is the desire for Intellectual pleasure or our want for non-material things and knowledge.

Dharma ——————— This is the desire for Spiritual pleasure and the want to know God.

Moska ——————— This is the desire for Spiritual Liberation or Enlightenment. The spirit wants to be free from the limitations of

the mind.

This is the beginning of the path where we may also find fear from lack of material things. We generally then move from fear to anger and adopt a need for power and control. Once power is maintained then one generally looks inward in search of realization. These are the first steps on our path where we slowly start to make choices that move from being selfish to being selfless.

In the root chakra, we find our instinctual desires and the formation of primal life. This chakra is located in the Coccyx at the base of the spine, which is close to the perineum. In order to strengthen this chakra and raise dormant energy, we must bring this chakra into balance. We must not be controlled by our base desires. We must attain self-mastery and tell our bodies what to do rather than having our bodies telling us what to do. We do these things to learn to conserve energy and strengthen our aura so that we don't create holes and lose unnecessary amounts of energy through various actions related to the vrittis. This center represents earth as its element. When this center is strong it helps in the formation of solid matter in your body. It's said to increase the strength of your bones, and even create a pleasant scent in a person with a balanced root chakra. A balanced root chakra is also associated with bowel health.

-Sacral Chakra – Svadhisthana (Orange) I feel
Element: Water
Symbolic Animal: Crocodile

This center is related to our lizard brain. This has to do with the base structure in our brain which is the same as a reptile. This chakra or energy center is known to be responsible for the liquid element in the body and is associated with the lymphatic system. The 6 petals, or vrittis, are as follows:

Avajina ———— Disdain for others
Murccha ——— Stupor or frozen depression
Prashraya —— Gluttony or over consumption
Avishvasa—— Distrust in others

Sarvanasha — The fear of death
Krurata ——— Indifference or mercilessness

These propensities are emotional states that we must overcome. They determine if we balance this chakra through love, and channel energy further upward, or if we are to feed our reptilian tendencies and move downward into the physical realm of deterioration.

This chakra is connected with our addictions. Often when we do not find the satisfaction we seek in this material life, we are left feeling empty, knowing there is something more. We often fill that emptiness with anything we can. Moderation is key to the development of this center. It is very important to save your vital life fluids and not to waste semen. When this center is balanced it is said that the person will have a glow to them and increase their attractiveness. Remember, our energetic expression becomes our physical expression.

-Solar Plexus Chakra – Manipura (Yellow) I Do
Element: Fire
Symbolic Animal: Ram

This center is responsible for generating heat in the body and proper digestion. The solar plexus chakra is also connected with our mammalian tendencies. We see that as we move up the spine we go from primal to spiritual. Still, we find base instincts here that we must overcome. These are the vrittis that we must conquer in this center.

lajja ————— Shame or bashfulness
pishunata —— Greed
iirsya ————-Jealousy or envy
susupti ———-Sleepiness or laziness
visada———— Melancholy or sadness
kasaya———— Cruelty or sadistic tendencies
trsna———— Thirst or infatuation
moha———— Attachment to the physical
ghrna———— Hatred

bhhaya————————- Fear

One of the most important tendencies that we must overcome in this chakra is our attachment to material things. This also includes attachment to people. Most of our pain and fear comes from attachment. We have to lose our lust for material things. Only in this way do we achieve true freedom. Attachment and love are not the same thing. Attachment comes from time and proximity. The longer something is around you the more we tend to become attached. So how do we overcome attachment and still maintain love? Well, we must love the essence of all things and not the form. We can easily become attached to form, but this is not true love, it is closer to addiction.

Cold showers are good for this chakra as they help the body maintain its ability to self-heat and self regulate. Also, a vegetarian diet is recommended as digestion is easier and takes less energy, and without meat and fat content the blood vessels don't get restricted which can cause health problems when stress is introduced. If you're going all-in avoid alcohol and tobacco.

-Heart Chakra – Anahata (Green) I Love
Element: Air
Symbolic Animal: Antelope

The heart chakra is the central gateway between the spiritual and the material worlds. The 3 chakras below represent our inhumanity. The heart chakra represents our humanity, And the 3 chakras above represent divinity. Only a person who acts through their heart can ascend to being divine. Here we have 12 petals or tendencies of this center, some to embody and some to avoid.

Asha————————- Hope
Cinta————————- Morality
Cesta————————— Effort
Mamta————————— Love
Dhamba———————— Arrogance, vanity
Viveka———————— Discrimination between right and wrong
Vikalata————————- Depression, or Languor

Ahamkara ——- Ego and Pride
Lolata ————- Extreme acquisition or avarice
Kapatata ——-— Hypocrisy
Vitarka ———— Argumentativeness
Anutapa ———- Regret

The heart chakra is associated with the thymus. This organ in the neck is responsible for creating T-cells and maintaining our immune system. Unconditional love is always the answer to any problem. We create joy in service to others, and find depression when we only serve ourselves. One way we can strengthen this center is to dance and do good deeds whenever you see the opportunity. Breathing through the heart with love is a great way to balance this center. Meditation in groups is also very powerful at charging this center and bringing it into balance.

-Throat Chakra – Vishuddha (White or Blue) I Talk
Element: Ether or Akasha
Symbolic Animal: White Elephant

The throat chakra is where we first begin to see divinity. This center is represented by ether, or space and time because sound is the most subtle physical force we have. It is not a thing at all, but rather, a pressure wave. These petals are slightly different than the other centers, as this chakra encompasses mantras and seed sounds or vowels.

Mantras
Pranava —— Ohm Mantra
Udgitha ——- Samaveda Mantras
Hung———— Bij Mantra
Phat ————- Bij Mantra
Vashat ———— Mantra
Svadha ——— Mantra
Svah ——— Mantra
Namah ——— Mantra
Amrita ——— Nectar of immortality (likely Melatonin, but potentially something else)

Musical Notes / Vowels (Sanskrit)
Nishda————लृ(lr)
Rishabha———ए(e)
Gandhara——ऐ(ai)
Shadja————ओ(o)
Madhyama——औ(au)
Dhalvata———आ(aa)
Panchama———-अ(a)

It is said that the fields of chi resonate with a sound, and that sound is om. This sound encompasses all existence. In India, it is "aum" while in China it is "om"

The first sound in this mantra the "a" stands for the first word spoken and the start of existence. The second sound "o" stands for all of time and creation. And finally, the sound "m" stands for dissolution and the end of existence.

The mantra "om ma ne pad me om" means I know that the divine energy of all resides dormant in my root chakra. The use of mantras is indeed a method of attaining higher states of consciousness. What happens is that not only are you sending energy out that you wish to match up with, but you are repeating a phrase to the point that your analytical left side of the brain gets bored and stops paying attention, and your right hemisphere can then take over and begin leading the way to an elevated state. Not only can sound bring you closer to the divine, but it is vital in our expression, and the determination of whether we climb up to unity with God, or if our actions keep us in the mundane.

Singing can help balance this chakra as well as speaking truth and compassion. Breathing with focused intent through this chakra will help to strengthen it. The development up to this center is known to be associated with the manifestation of several siddhis, or superhuman abilities.

-Third Eye Chakra – Ajna (purple or indigo) I See
Element: Supreme Element (all elements combined)
Symbolic Animal: Black Antelope

The third eye is the center that generally gets the most attention. This center, being above those below it, is in control of, and can regulate all of the descending chakras. The third eye chakra is connected with the hypothalamus. This organ located in our brains literally controls, spiritually and physically, the other chakras below. The hypothalamus produces hormones regulating emotional responses. It also plays a key role in maintaining body temperature and several daily unconscious processes while simultaneously controlling other areas such as sexual desire and appetite. So in a sense, if you can bring this energy center into balance you will bring all of the centers below into balance as well. The 2 petals around this chakra are focused on knowledge.
Knowledge of the physical
Knowledge of the spiritual

The third eye is the center for knowledge of all things. It represents not only the ability to learn everything from the physical world but it also gives us the ability to discover all information from the spiritual world. When one looks outward they see the material existence, and when they look inward they find divinity. A person must develop this center to progress further up the path to enlightenment. At this point, a person who is dedicated has mostly changed their views from a dualistic perspective to a non-dualistic perspective and lives as if they are the world. They live a life with unconditional love for everything. If someone else is suffering, then you must see them like they are yourself. You must raise your consciousness to the level of god's consciousness, and from here you can begin to do his work and raise humanity to their rightful divine intended state. With this center, you will develop your intuition and direct knowing. Things like remote viewing and blindfolded sight can be refined to a level that can rehabilitate the blind and see clearly into the akashic records like

you are watching the past on a tv. From this point, you can now clearly understand God's intention and connect with the source of all infinite consciousness. Meditating deeply on, "I am," helps this center. Also sun-gazing has been know to clear out third eye. Be sure to only sun-gaze during the first hour of sunrise or during the final hour before sunset. This is when the UV rays are low enough to be beneficial and not damaging.

-Crown Chakra – (Violet) I Understand
Element: Pure Consciousness
Symbolic Animal: Egg
1,000 pedals.

50x2x10=1,000. The 50 petals on all the chakras below, times 2 for the positive and negative expressions of them, times 10 which is a reference to the energy lay lines that extend out from our crown chakra. one going up, one going down, and the other eight going around us and out like a compass, N, NE, E, SE, S, SW, W, NW. These energy lines also come into play with the alignment of the pyramids as well as other practices like Feng Shui. These energetic systems are apparent and understood as the science that they are when the person has developed themselves energetically and can perceive the chakras directly.

The crown chakra represents the king of kings, god all mighty. This center is your true connection to the divine and resides above your head. This center is associated with the pineal gland in the center of the brain which is able to produce DMT and melatonin. There is a yogic substance that is said to be secreted by the pineal gland that is partially spiritual in nature, and if someone is not in the right state of meditation, the compound is assumed to be immediately destroyed. This still undiscovered secretion is called amrita, or the elixir of immortality, referenced in yogic culture. Many people believe that this elixir of life is actually referring to melatonin. One of the pineal gland's main functions is to determine if it's day or night and then to secrete the appropriate hormones. When it is the day, serotonin is produced, and we are put in a very awake state. When it is night, and less light enters

our eyes, then our pineal gland begins producing melatonin. Melatonin is known for having a sedative effect on the person. It will reduce stress levels and help a person attain higher states of meditation. Melatonin is produced around 9 pm and increases in levels until a maximum point around 12 pm. Many yogis recognize that higher levels of melatonin lead to deeper and more profound states of meditation. This is why between 12 am and 3 am it is recognized as the time of shiva, a time which has mystical properties. Interestingly enough, hunger can also increase the levels of melatonin. This is another reason fasting is utilized. It's also said that fasting with water is good for the body, and fasting without water is good for the body and the spirit.

An interesting study found that rats that were injected with melatonin had lower levels of stress and lived 20% longer than rats that weren't injected. Melatonin is a powerful antioxidant and has very beneficial anti-aging effects. Rumi has mentioned that meditation on this center, with unconditional love for the supreme being, and the oneness of all, leaves the person in a state of divine drunkenness.

Many of the Yogic sciences have been kept highly secret for generations. Yoga in Tibet is only passed down from master to student orally and they never write it down. Many enlightened masters have come from India, so we should pay attention to what these methods have to teach us. I have not mentioned any asanas in this book because in the west they have become the main focus while the actual science of spirit has been largely overlooked. Each different yoga posture will help in moving blood, twisting, bending, and stretching out the given area, or chakra. Because yoga is all about balancing the mind and the body a vegetarian diet is recommended so that you do not create any blockages in blood circulation or any vasoconstriction. Remember your body is your spirit, and if we want to attain we need to bring not only our bodies but our minds into balance and harmony so that they may work how they were intended.

CHAPTER 7: THE TREE OF LIFE

The Hidden Science

The Kabbalah is not a religion. It predates religion. The Kabbalah is also known as the hidden science, which was passed down orally. Its origin is shrouded in mystery, but the first accounts of the books show up around 4,000 years ago. Some believe it began in Spain, and others believe it comes from Israel and Abraham. This knowledge and science come from those who have become Ascended Masters or Kabbalists and learned the secrets of the universe. It is said that this knowledge was hidden for 6,000 years until man was at the right development to receive it properly. That time is now, and in 1995 all of the books that make up the Kabbalah have been made public. For centuries they have been hidden and shrouded in secrets and code. These books were written in a language of branches, a language within a language so that only those who were worthy and had a teacher would be able to gain the true knowledge the books had to offer. This is what I believe the rapture is, not a sudden random chosen few to raise to heaven. But rather the knowledge for us, as a collective whole, is now brought back into the light to help us raise our consciousness to realize the 4th-dimensional beings that we are, and how to actualize that reality. Our time to attain enlightenment is now. We must raise back up to the point we once were a million years ago in Shambhala times, referenced in Vedic scriptures.

What is Kabbalah?

The Kabbalah is the science of creation and ascension. It is said to be the science of all there is. It is known as the Tree of Life and has been adopted by many religions over time with references found in Judaism, Christianity, Buddhism, and the Hermetic sciences. Because of this, we find several different spellings like Cabala, Kabbalah, and Qabalah. It has been linked with Tarot cards, and many believe the 22 paths of the Kabbalah represent the 22 cards of the major arcana. We will be focusing on the Hebru variation of the Tree of Life as it is believed to be the original version. The Kabbalah was written in Aramaic and predates Jesus, and is fundemental in his true teachings on God and the workings of the universe. The Kabbalah differs from mosts religions, in the regard that, God in the Kabbalah is all perfect and all good. In many religions, it's perceived that God has an attitude, and we must fear him. In many faiths, it calls for us to beg and plead to god so that he may show mercy to us. This is not how it is in the Kabbalah, but rather God is unchanging and pure love. He only loves and pushes us all to learn and grow. God in the Kabbalah is not a separate entity that is outside of you, but instead, God is apart of you. He is all things ever created. In the Kabbalah, there are only 2 things, God and his creation, and they are 1.

Another Map to Enlightenment

The Tree of Life is yet another map of ascension similar to the chakra system we explored in the previous section. The Tree of Life is a very specific instruction manual on how to learn to interact with the forces of the divine that are hidden from most of humanity. This relates to blindfolded sight which is a vital key for developing spiritual skills and exploring existence beyond the physical. The sixth sense is our direct connection to the spirit realm, and one of our first steps to spiritual development with learning about who we truly are. The Tree of Life, when looked at from above, and descending to the bottom, shows the path of creation and God's divine will in action, manifesting a being in

physical form. And transversely, when we look at the Tree of Life, starting at the bottom going up, we see God's most solid form of matter and creation. From the lowest point ascending we see the path of life from the most basic level of inanimate things to vegetative, animal, and speaking life. Then there is the first barrier where we must learn a new sixth sense to pass, then we continue upward through 2 revelations until the final union with the creator in form. The Kabbalah is a how-to guide on becoming an enlightened master and conquering death.

When we listen to what some of the Kabbalists have to say about the spirit world, it leads to some pretty massive implications, and potentially explains how things like teleportation, by the Masters, is possible and achieved. The Kabbalistic theory says that all of humanity is a collective consciousness. Like a polop on coral, each one is living its own separate experience and yet they are part of one life. We also know from Steven Greer, and new theories in astrophysics, quantum psychics, and from enlightened masters, that there is another dimension or potentially many that we can phase into. Another interesting aspect of the Kabbalistic texts is that they describe a sort of programming through stages of life. I believe it should be interpreted as learning and can likely be related to the morphic field theory, which transcends life and death. In very many regards our existence is indeed similar to a holographic reality, but not to the level that some believe. Yes, everything is energy directed by intention, visualization, and information, but everything is also real. Spirit is matter, and yet matter is more like a dream. Reincarnation is real, we only die to come back and do better until we learn to stop dying. One other important aspect that is similar to the holographic theory is that every piece of this whole existence we are in contains the whole, similar to that of a hologram. Change one piece, and you change the whole board to reflect that piece.

Huge Implications

The Kabbalists tell us that the spirit world sits in a place outside of time and space. This I believe is the fields of chi and

the akashic records, as chi exists out of the bounds of time and space and is the place that matter arises from. The Masters tell us that to travel in these dimensions of the spirit, we must align our thoughts and feelings with where we want to go. And in this way, which describes the exact art and science of manifestation, we can travel and increase our proximity to the desired location. This is the main method of application that one would use to ascend to higher spiritual levels, by trying to understand and do as God does. The closer this alignment, the greater the connection, and a larger amount of light can enter the vessel. I believe this also has immense implications for exactly how material things are brought forth from the invisible, just as Jesus did with the loaves of bread. This also explains the method of astral travel, and at higher levels, how one would be able to manifest a second body to work through, as many masters do.

There is a law that is referenced in, *The Life and Teachings of the Masters of the Far East* over and over again. It is referenced as, the one perfect law that, through its application the masters can perform what many would call miracles but they refer to as exact science that is replicable with the proper actions. I believe that this is the Law of Equivalence of Form as referenced in the teachings of the Kabbalah. This law states that there are constant forces from the inside and the outside of everything that are pushing things into balance. The inner forces being our divine nature and the spiritual, and the outer forces being our environment and the physical. As humans we have been predominantly cut off from our connection with the spiritual forces in existence, so we do not utilize this law. The Kabbalah teaches us that everything that is formed came from the spirit first, and nothing happens in the physical without happening first in the spiritual. By the use of this law with the perfection of energy use by the Master, as well as perfection of their sixth sense and visualization, they can manifest bread, making it in physical form from the spiritual. The perfect fulfillment of the law means the bread is then brought forth into the physical and appears out of what seems like thin air.

The Purpose of Life

The Tree of Life shows us that the entire purpose of creation, was so that God could create a being and fill it with unbounded joy. In doing this God created a vessel, separate and yet one, which was brought forth as a being of reception. God only gives, and we were designed to receive. As we progress up the tree from formal creation we see that our will to receive slowly shrinks and our will to give increases. Matter is spirit, and we are in the spirit world as much as we are in the physical one. By changing our will from receiving to giving, we grow our spiritual connection with God and our proximity in spirit. We slowly become more and more beings of light as we make our corrections in life and live as intended. The Kabbalah is meant to teach people how to enter the spirit world and make all of our final corrections in one lifetime, so that we never die again, and attain the highest bliss.

So we are the will to receive, how do we change to the will to give? First, we must accept that we are the will to receive and understand that by receiving we can give even more. By attaining ourselves we can spread the light even more. One important aspect the Kabbalists speak about is that more than actions, it's the intention that matters. You have to bring your understanding to God's level and see beyond good and evil. Everything is perfection. We have free will to do anything we wish, and from this we created duality, and the Tree of life shows us that the way to ascension is recognizing our divinity and trying to be pure love for all and see the good in even the worst events. When plants die, they add to the soil and grow the next generation stronger and more vibrant than was possible origionally. We are a collective. One of the most fundamental goals of these teachings is to show man that the greatest joy and perfection comes from giving to others and treating your neighbor as yourself. We must treat every other person we see like us, and want to help them and bring them comfort and satisfaction as much as we do for ourselves. This is the path to godliness where one can align with his spiritual energies and become a being that is more and more light.

We are all in this together, and only by working together as one will we all ascend. But all of this must be done for the betterment of all and God, and not for a person's ego. Transcending the ego is a vital factor for immortality. "Carved (harut) on the stones. Do not pronounce it, Carved (harut) but rather, freedom (herut). To show that they are freed from the angel of death." (Midrash Shmot Raba, 41)

The path to ascension is said to lead to great doubt, and this is on purpose. You must not do this for yourself, but rather for all mankind. You cannot be selfish, you must be selfless. There are said to be 125 steps beyond the first barrier into the spirit world to reach unity with God. These steps are also related to genes that activate and change a person as they ascend the Tree of Life. The path is walked only by taking the middle way similar to Taoism. It must be taken out of free will and altruism.

The 10 Sefirot

Top
Keter (nothingness or God)
Hokhmah (The Divine Father of Knowledge)
Binah (The Divine Mother of Creation)
Hesed (Loving Kindness)
Din (Justice)
Tif'eret (Mans soul)
Nezah (Eternity or Victory)
Hod (Glory or Splendor)
Yesod (Foundation)
Shekhinah (Mans physical world, The elements, and gods presence in the world)
Bottom

The 4 factors:

There are also 4 factors mentioned in the Kabbalah. These factors apply both to the spiritual and the physical sides of existence.

1. The bed (something from nothing, a seed)
2. The conduct of cause and effect, related to the bed's attribute, which in reality, remains unchanged. (death is to grow)
3. The internal cause and effect, that change as a result of contact with alien(or external) forces. (to be reconstituted in better form with added hidden forces. Like how one plant can create soil for better plants that couldn't have come before)
4. The cause and effect of alien forces acting completely from the outside (we are searching for the end of correction in one lifetime, a book for example can spark inner change)

—

5 States of Attainment

1. Double concealment (Feels there is no god or reason for anything.)
2. Single concealment (Believes there is a reason for everything. May learn and begin preparation by using a book or guide.)
—————(After this state, is the barrier to the spiritual world.)
3. Correction (Satisfaction comes from all things and more giving leads to more success, your sixth sense is developed here as well.)
4. First revelation (High level of contact with the creators nature. Sees and wants and feels the same as the creator. You must learn how to respond in every situation, this teaches you where you are)
5. Second revelation (Reaching equivalence of form with the creator. Love your friend as yourself. Live in harmony, working together towards the whole)

—

The degree to which we understand the perfection of all things and events by the creator constitutes the level of our connection with the creator. In action and thought when you are not aligned

with God he cannot provide for you, this is why we decay, age, and die. We are the will to receive, it's how we use it that matters.

So, in conclusion, to ascend in the spiritual realm and become one with God more fully so that we may attain enlightenment requires that we make our actions, thoughts, and feelings the same as god. We change ourselves to move to him in the timeless spaceless reality of the deeper nature of our world. For there is no other world, but that which we cannot perceive, or have not developed the sense to perceive.

Next, I want to include a quote from Jesus himself, recorded as he stood and spoke among a group of american researchers, while they traveled with other enlightened masters. This is from *The Life and Teachings of the Masters of the Far East Books.* What I've found is that the teachings of Jesus come directly from the Kabbalah, or the Tree of Life.

Jesus speaks, "When I said I am the way, the truth, and the light. I was not trying to convey that I myself am the only true light. As many are lead by the spirit of God, they are sons of God. When I said I am the perfect son, the only begotten son of God, in whom the father is well pleased. I fully intended to convey the thought to all mankind, that one of gods children saw, understood, and claimed his divinity. Saw that he lived, moved, and had his being in god, the great father/mother principle of all things. That seeing this, he then spoke forth the word that he is the Christ, the only begotten son of God, and with true heart and steadfast purpose, lived the light, becoming what he claimed to be. With his eyes fixed on that ideal, he filled his whole body with that ideal, and the end thought was fulfilled. The reason that so many have not seen me, is that they have put me up on a shrine, and placed me in the unapproachable. They have surrounded me with miracles and mysteries, and again they have placed me far from the common people whom I love dearly. I love them with a love that is unspeakable. I have not withdrawn from them, they have withdrawn from me. They have set up veils, walls, and partitions, me-

diators, and images of myself and those so near and dear to me. They have surrounded us with myth and mystery until we seem so far removed from these dear ones that they do not know how to approach. They pray and supplicate my dear mother and those around me, and thus, they hold us all in mortal thought. When truly, if they would know us as we are, they would and could shake our hands. If they would drop all superstition and creed, and know us as we are. They could talk with us as you do. We are no different, at any time, then as you see us. How we would love to have the whole world know this. Then, what an awakening, what a reunion, what a feast. You have surrounded us for so long in mystery, it is no wonder that doubt and disbelief have become dominant. The more you build images and idols, and surround us with death, and make us unapproachable, save for some other than ourselves, the deeper doubts' shadow will be cast, and the chasm of superstition grow wider and more difficult to cross. If you would boldly shake our hands and say, "I know you," then all could see and know us as we are. There is no mystery surrounding us or those we love, for we love the whole world. So many see only that part of my life which ended on the cross, forgetting that the greater part is as I am now. Forgetting that man still lives, even after what seems a violent death. Life cannot be destroyed, It goes on and on. And life, well lived, never degenerates, nor passes. Even the flesh may be immortalized so that it never changes. Dear pilot, when he washed his hands and said, "Away with him, crucify him yourself." I find no fault in him. How little he knew of the history he was making. Or of the prophecy, he was fulfilling. He, with a multitude, has suffered far more than I have suffered. That is all past and forgotten. Forgiven as you see by our all standing here in one place."

CHAPTER 8: THE REAL PURPOSE OF MEDITATION

Why Meditate?

For those who have attained they know meditation is a vital tool. For everyone else, we question what it's really about and why should I meditate anyway? Meditation is gaining more and more attention in neuroscientific research and is becoming popular for many with words like mindfulness. Just like yoga, meditation is much deeper than what is perceived in the west. In reality, there are 2 things that make up all existence, spirit and matter. When our eyes are open we live entirely in the physical world, focusing on its laws and forces and charting our way through its rugged terrain. When our eyes are closed, we plunge ourselves beneath the waters of the physical world and enter into the spirit. Everything that comes into form first comes from visualization in the spirit world. Our minds are like wild elephants running around without our control. The first step in gaining any control in your life for, any reason, is to gain control of your mind. You must make your own decisions, and not be guided by impulse or rash thinking. When you become a master of your mind you can master anything, even attain enlightenment.

Meditation in yoga is for connecting with the source of all things. It is for self-realization and the dismantling of the ego. Meditation is for unlocking siddhis and getting closer to God. Through

meditation, we can heal our bodies and unlock our sixth sense. We can gather energy and communicate telepathically. We can leave our bodies and soar through space in astral form. We are so much more than we believe and for many, the first step to realizing this, comes through meditation.

Step 1: Focus on Your Breath

The first step in meditating is to build your ability to focus and concentrate. So many people growing up never learned to properly concentrate and focus. We hardly pay attention to the things we are doing and make mistakes and try to multitask. This leads to more energy used often with a lower rate of success. It's hard for us to multitask, as we can't truly focus on two things at once. Our attention only switches from one to the other and back again leaving larger room for error. A great test for concentration is to take a post-it, with a dot on it, and place it on the wall. Then, attempt to stare at the post-it for as long as you can, you will find how quickly we will distract ourselves from our original objective.

Improving your focus corresponds with physiological changes in the brain. You simply meditate and focus on the feeling of the breath entering and leaving through the rims of your nostrils. This builds your ability to focus, by constantly bringing your attention back to your breath and letting thoughts go, emptying your mind. This is what people call mindfulness and it does help in many areas. You lower the chatter in your brain and build control over your will. The prefrontal cortex becomes more active when we bring ourselves back into the now, and not thinking of the past or the future. By doing this we are making new neural pathways and training old ones to allow us better performance with less energy. Our intuition and our response time improve, as well as our memory and concentration. The hypocampus also begins to gain more control over what's called the default mode network. This is how we can begin to gain more control over areas of the brain that are active when we are at rest.

Our brains have high neuroplasticity, which means they are chan-

ging all the time, whether we do it on purpose or not. Much of the time this happens without our knowledge. For example, when raising children, it's almost more important to show them the right thing to do rather than telling them. We are very empathetic and because of our mirror neurons, we reflect the emotions and situations we encounter in life. This concept is also very important to children around 7 and 8 as this is where they will begin building their views of the world and their place in it. Young children under the ages of 12 are often in theta and delta brainwave states. Theta is the programming state of consciousness, where we can speak directly to the subconscious without any mental barriers that fact check and question the incoming information.

Healing Brain Damage

A large percentage of people who come back from war, are in prison, or in the NFL with anger issues, may have have a neurological issue they are unaware of. The good news is that our brains can be healed due to their high neuroplasticity. we can truly rehabilitate people in prison but we don't. Meditation and compassion change the structure of the brain itself. Brain damage can be reversed on a brain smart program as mentioned by Daniel Amen in his ted talk. This is also related to things like ADHD. We can train people to learn how to focus and improve their lives in nearly every way. Many of these things seem invisible but with spectral imaging of the brain, we can see them more clearly. Daniel Amen made a good point when he said that psychology is the only medical profession that doesn't look at the organ in question when making a diagnosis.

Delta

There are several brainwave states that we all experience in our lives. The lowest frequency with the highest amplitude is delta, which is between .5 Hz and 4 Hz. This state is normally associated with sleeping and healing. This is where things like our autonomic nervous system shine. When we are in deep states of delta

sleep, it is often dreamless, and our neurons are shut off throughout the body from gamma-aminobutyric acid (GABA). This state is not limited to dreamless sleep but has also been a path to gamma brainwaves, reported by Joe Dispenza's findings, which also show links to transcendental and religious experiences.

Theta

Next, we have theta brainwaves, moving up in frequency and down in amplitude. Theta is generally between 5 Hz and 8 Hz (or cycles per second). Theta is known as a drowsy state where you can access your subconscious and deep memories you think you've forgotten. Theta is where true hypnosis takes place. You can program your subconscious ideas and perceptions here. You can overcome fears and anxieties. One thing we should all be aware of is that if it's a battle of ideas between our subconscious and our conscious mind. The subconscious will always win. This state is also a state that one would be in for things like a shamanic journey. In this brainwave state, we also find the Schumman resonance. The Schumman resonance is the earth's resonant frequency which oscillates at 7.83 Hz. This can change depending on solar radiation, which has geomagnetic effects on the earth. This resonance and frequency are where a person can tune into the earth, and everything on it, as you would tune into a radio. Most of the realities of remote viewing and remote influencing are found to be performed at this level. This is also why, when there are geomagnetic storms or solar flares, a person's ability to remote view can disrupted. Theta is where visualization can also become vivid and detailed.

Alpha

Alpha is the state of inspiration and imagination. This state is generally found between 8 Hz and 13 Hz. When you are watching a movie or listening to music you are often in the alpha state. Alpha is a state where light hypnosis may be performed as well as early states of meditation. Alpha is also one of the states that we use in extrasensory perception abilities and the feeling of subtle the energies.

Beta

Then moving up in frequency and lower in aptitude we have beta brainwaves between 14 Hz and 30-39 Hz. These are associated with normal daily functions and are found when we are doing things like working. This is when we are fully alert and aware.

Gamma

Stepping up one more level we begin to get into the superconscious. gamma brainwaves are measured at levels above 40 Hz, gamma brainwaves occur in people when they have done something like bitten into an orange or come up with the solution to a difficult problem. Gamma brainwaves are also recorded when people perform telekinesis. Astonishingly most people do not reach the levels of coherence and synchronicity that Tibetan monks achieve. When first studying brainwaves the classification of gamma didn't become a thing until olympic level meditators began getting brain scans. These were people who had over 62,000 lifetime hours of meditation. The first thing they noticed was how different their brainwaves were from ours. These people just live throughout their day in gamma brainwaves. And even more interestingly, when these meditators focused on compassion, their gamma brainwaves would jump up 700-800%. This suggests there is a higher state of consciousness that most people never really achieve. After asking these monks what this state feels like, they describe it as being spacious and open and ready for anything. Often scientists haven't had the proper EEG devices to measure the full extent and range of these high-level meditators.

Influencing Gene Expression

Meditation can have profound effects on the body. We gain more control over our minds and our body. We can also influence gene expression. There are very interesting things being done with Evelyn at, Seeing Without Eyes. They have found that you can do things like influence stem cells for growing new teeth for example. We see that negative emotions affect stress and can

degrade our body's functions. Often we overlook the fact that positive emotions have positive effects as well. Much of our gene expression comes from our interaction with the environment which the body perceives through emotions and feelings. By doing things like meditating on elevated emotions we can activate many of these laden biological functions. You can promote healing in your body with thought and emotion.

With practice, we gain more control over our amygdala and reign in this elephant of a mind we have. We can master stress and anxiety this way. Breathwork is another fantastic tool we can use in conjunction with meditation that allows us to accomplish some of these same goals. With meditation comes increased levels of melatonin which is a strong antioxidant and helps in preventing aging. Our DNA also gains more protection as the length of our telomeres grows leading to longevity. This has a lot to do with how our immune cells age.

In the long run, many of us lose brain cells as we get older, but we can learn to grow more through meditation. One Harvard study found that after 8 weeks of meditation the subjects had grown more neurons, increased the size of the gray matter in their brains, and increased the weight of their brains. The physical structure is changed through meditation and operations become more efficient. Not only that but you end up improving the strength and amplitude of your brainwaves. Often one will go down into a theta brainwave state and stay awake allowing the body to come into harmony, and the brain begins to produce more energy at higher wavelengths.

The CIA's Research

When the CIA researched astral projection and transcendental meditation they found some very interesting things. In the Gateway process, they utilized three main forms of practice. Hypnosis, Biofeedback, and transcendental meditation.

Hypnosis

Through hypnosis, they found they were able to access the sen-

sory-motor cortex, the pleasure centers, and the lower cerebral sections of the right side of the brain. They were able to speak directly to the right side of the brain which is responsible for imagination, feelings, and the majority of spiritual phenomena, without the left, analytical, logical, language side of the brain interceding in any way. This was used primarily to allow for quicker progress through the program by removing fears and establishing the reality of possibility. Also by giving the listener enhanced confidence, concentration, and focus.

Biofeedback

Then there is biofeedback which uses both sides of the brain together to achieve the desired result with the practitioner able to see, and correct mistakes. This is especially helpful when a meditator can see their brainwaves or hear a noise letting them know where they are. Biofeedback can help strengthen neurological pathways that allow us to take conscious control over unconscious actions. For example, pain can be blocked out and healing can be enhanced. This is very helpful with new meditators and greatly improves their advancement.

Trancendental Meditation

And finally, we have transcendental meditation which ignores the left side of the brain so that we can interact with the right. Things like mantras are repeated until the left side of the brain gets bored and the right side can take over. The CIA studied transcendental meditation in terms of Kundalini awakenings. They were able to measure the movement of energy through, what's known in the east as, the microcosmic orbit of chi. This was seen when energy was pulled up the spine to the head producing acoustical waves that were conducted in the subject's grey matter in their brain. These waves were from the heart and formed a rhythm called the bifurcation echo. This echo is like a pressure wave that moves up and down in the body like a slinky wave bouncing from one end to another. When we meditate and our body is in tune and this echo reverberates as the heartbeats in a

smooth rhythm. The body then works in harmony like a tuned instrument. This echo is audible and heard up to 3 times louder than the normal heartbeat. The raising of the Kundalini is something that takes around 5 years of meditation and practice. This is something even highly regarded among yogis. The CIA found that these energy movements could be produced in people using vibrations or frequencies. It was noted that with binaural beats Kundalini awakenings could be achieved sooner than without. People with sensitive nervous systems were also susceptible to random Kundalini awakenings due to mechanical or auditory vibrations for protracted periods between 4-7hz. This, for example, could be from an air conditioner or while in a car traveling over a certain part of the road and speed creates just the right vibrations.

Binaural Beats

Binaural beats were discovered by the Monroe Institute as a means to get the right and left hemispheres to synchronize. They called their new sound technology Hemi-sync. This utilizes two different frequencies played in each ear. One frequency for example could be 100 Hz in the right ear and 108 Hz in the left ear. Even though there are two separate oscillations of sounds coming in your ears your brain will take the two and create a third that is not on the tape at 4 Hz. Your brain has to actively have the left and the right hemispheres sync up to produce what you hear. This is how they were able to induce a resonate frequency at such low tones as 4 Hz and still be registered by our hearing. The brain then tries to match up and tune in with whatever frequency it is perceiving which allows sound to help bring us through different states of consciousness. One of the main goals of the Gateway project was to bring subjects down into relaxed states around the Schumann resonance for astral projection and remote viewing. There are different levels mentioned in the Monroe Project. Different levels of attainment and advancement. These levels progress up in what's called "focuses." Advanced techniques begin to arise like traveling to the past after focus 10 moving up to

focus 21 which is looking into the future. They say that only 4% of those who train make it past focus 15. Progression through these focuses was directly linked to the time people put in. Here is an idea of what some of this process looks like. This is from de-classified documents made available due to the freedom of information act.

The Gateway Process

The Gateway Process (Astral Projection & Advanced Energy States)A. Begin by using Hemi-sync tapes.B. Add strong rem sleep frequencies.C. Provide hypnosis for easier and deeper states of hypnosis.D. Use hypnosis for more states of focus and concentration to progress rapidly through the next exercises.E. Repeat steps A-C with the suggestion that an outer body movement will be acquired and remembered even after sleep ends.F. Repeat E to control out of body movement even after rem sleep ends.G. Encourage the pursuit of all self-knowledge and remove any blockages to progress.H. Be prepared to encounter intelligent forces.I. Encourage advanced participants to build energy fields, for advances in attainment, to help others learn and assist them.

How to Produce DMT

Meditation is also vital for developing Blindfolded Sight and achieving higher states of focus and energy output. This is how we expand our consciousness and allow for the formation of other abilities. This is how you open your third eye. When we have our eyes closed we can begin to see color and lights through the production of DMT in your pineal gland. We must go through the darkness to see the light. Mantak Chia tells us about how in the Tao, as a practice, they put people into a completely dark room for a week. This allows our brains to produce more and more melatonin which then converts to 5-MeO DMT. After the first and second day, the melatonin levels slowly increase up to 5mlg and up until they reach around 25mlg when DMT begins to be produced. Mantak tells us about how on the second and third day the levels are getting high enough that the people in the

dark will begin seeing their past lives and their spirit will want to leave their bodies. This is how they develop their astral projection abilities as well as awakening their sixth sense. I've also heard several people tell me about native tribes who would take their children and raise them for a short period in the complete darkness of a cave to develop their sixth sense. I have not personally found references for this but I have been told about it several times now. This does make perfect sense. To begin conscious DMT production we must meditate or simply spend enough time in the pitch-black darkness. This similar method is also referenced by Sadhguru who said that, to activate your third eye, one needs at least 36 hours of meditation. Unfortunately with age, our melatonin levels tend to drop so these states are often more easily attained by younger generations.

Meditation is so much more powerful than we realize. Not only does it unlock superconscious states and supernatural abilities with ESP, but it can help us in all aspects of life. Meditation has been shown to reduce cancer growth and mitigates radiation from chemotherapy. It increases your body's natural killer cells and protects your DNA. It reduces fat content in the body and can help with diabetes. It is shown to help in producing neural protective hormones and can help with Parkinson's and Alzheimer's. It also reduces the damage of brain injuries.

Our world is full of random aspects that are constantly being influenced by our minds and energy. This is seen in binary quantum entanglement when we use our intention to affect random number generators or even things like the PH in water, or even the flow of wind. You may have noticed your interconnection with the world around you through things like the radio or tv answering questions that come across your mind. Our aura interacts with the world around us at a deeper level than most can see.

Your Aura

Your electromagnetic energy field, produced by the heart, grows or shrinks depending on your emotional state. We can strengthen and widen our electromagnetic field through things like compas-

sion meditation. This field is also seen as a field of protection by high-level yogis. The larger the field, the greater the protection. Our fields interact with each other whether we are aware or not. You see this when couples are close together their heartbeats will sync up. This is where we can get a feeling that someone is behind us or that someone is looking at us. It's been shown that you can put two people in separate rooms and have them be unaware of the other person. But through the wall, their auras will interact and cause physiological changes in the subjects. When a person is sad, their field may only stretch out 3 feet around them. When a person is happy their fields can stretch out up to 20 feet around them affecting everyone who comes in contact with their field. This explains vibes, and can also be related to the chakra system, showing us how energy, strength, and resilience comes from love and conviction. This is also why many Masters avoid crowds and lots of people, their fields would be slowly drained simply by being around those who are leaking and constantly losing energy.

CHAPTER 9: ARE JEDI REAL? YES, AND SO IS THE FORCE

Every ability that a Jedi has, we can also train. Telekinesis, telepathy, levitation, blindfolded sight, everything is real from a superhuman ability standpoint, except for the lightsaber...yet. You've heard of Tibetan sound levitation before. Many monks surrounding a bolder with long horns chanting and singing mantras. This too is real. The force, in Star Wars, would be interpreted as ether or chi, which pervades all things and exists outside of space and time. This is the field that connects all things. The Jedi religion has been gaining popularity recently and it stems from concepts in Taoism, Zen Buddhism, and from the Samurai.

Often we see people spinning psywheels with their minds and their energy. This is only the beginning. Without dedication and understanding, people often don't get past this. Energy is real and is sensed through our nervous system, and generated in a variety of forms. It is ideal to train the body using yogic breathing techniques and slow dynamic movement optimizing our system. Then one would need to train the mind using meditation for a variety of purposes. A few of which are to increase the size of the electromagnetic field around your body as well as improving your brainwave strength and amplitude. Then you would need to train your spirit which is the force. Here you would grow your energy through the first two steps and refine your senses and energy

manipulation abilities. The three are needed, mind, body, and spirit.

Humanity today is disconnected from their higher self, or the force. In religion, they would call this God, or the holy ghost, but someone spiritual may say, the universe, source, or their higher self. All of these are the same thing, and we may figure out some-day that chi is actually dark matter too. That would be crazy, and that's also just a guess based on a show I'm watching called, "His Dark Materials". Interesting stuff. Chi is the zero-point energy field from which all matter comes into being. This is the base of our existence.

Improving your extrasensory perception is vital for understand-ing and communicating with the force. Information after all is energy, and this field of chi is intelligent. When moving down the path of spirituality and forming a connection with your higher self and source love is the most powerful energy there is. This is the way, unconditional love for all. You must see your neighbor as yourself and treat everyone how you want to be treated. This is the only way a person can fully commune with, and master the force, for the force is love. It is the binding energy that holds mat-ter into existence forming physical representations of energy.

As we've learned in the previous articles to move closer to some-thing in the spirit world, or in the psychic realm (chi). We must bring our thoughts and feelings closer to the vibration of what we are trying to connect with. So for us to connect with source and we must learn unconditional love for all and understand the per-fection in all things. This is how we become more spiritual and connect with our higher self. The underlying fabric of existence is not based in time or space, so our mind is the only way we can move. Remember, all points in space and time are one.

It is our responsibility to create the world that we want to see in the future. Meditation is not just for mindfulness, it is for connecting with source, generating energy, astral projection, and so much more. We have to teach the next generation that these things are not imaginary or fake but with the proper training, we are literally capable of anything that we put our minds to. Blind-

folded sight and developing your internal screen, third eye, or sixth sense will be vital for our future. As Tesla said, "The day science begins to study non-physical phenomena, it will make more progress in one decade than in all the previous centuries of its existence."

In Indonesia, we see old traditions that have not faded or been put on the back burner. Kings and Queens recently ruled there, and with that, we had ancient traditions and secrets that are the basis for most of our superhero myths. Many of the legends are true, and we have forgotten our history. There is potential evidence that we have had ancient, great civilizations, millions of years ago, that lived utilizing a higher technology that we have not figured out yet. This was the technology of consciousness and spirit. Without T.V.s and modern entertainment, people focused deeply on mystical things with real-world results.

In the 60's the Kings and Queens of central Java realized that their heritage of secrets teachings, if brought public, could give many blind people back their lives. Through an understanding of subtle energies and spirit, and with the right training in these fields, they have taught thousands of blind people how to see again. You don't even need eyes. Yes, this is very real, and we need to make this mainstream. We have an obligation to all future generations on earth, to provide the best possible chance, for the brightest possible future we can have. A future where people can fly and love is the answer to every question. I know it seems idealistic and you may think it's not possible. But we can, and we will.

This idea is also shared by Lt. Col. Jim Channon, founder of the First Earth Battalion in 1981. The First Earth Battalion was designed with the intention of creating super-soldiers, who were more like warrior monks, with capabilities allowing them to levitate, walk through walls, and remote influence people. Much of this came after reports showed that the Soviets were developing psychic abilities and had achieved things like, knocking people out or even killing them through the influence of thought. This whole story is portrayed pretty accurately in the movie, *The Men Who Stare At Goats*. I highly recommend you watch this

movie again and see it as an account of true events.

This was called Project Jedi. In this program, we find the title of the movie, *The Men Who Stare At Goats*. At Fort Bragg, in North Carolina, they had 100 goats in a rundown building with several men, staring at them, to try and kill them telepathically. These poor goats were repeatedly shot and mended for medical training purposes, and some even had their legs plastered in place. There is a man who managed to accomplish this task, and his name is Guy Savelli, the goat starer. Many of these stories are brought to light in the book, The Men Who Stare At Goats, by Jon Ronson. I highly recommend you check this book out as well.

The origins of the Jedi can even be traced back to Egyptian times when they were known as the Djed. There are conflicting stories debating whether this was a single man (Hermes Trismegistus/Thoth potentially responsible for the emerald tablets and/or the Corpus Hermeticum) or a group of magicians who had a deep understanding of the universe and its workings. I prefer to see them as a group as some of the stories relate even to ancient methods on how the pyramids were constructed. This may very well have been the inspiration for George Lucas when we came up with Star Wars. It's interesting to watch these movies and realize that much of them is very possible and achievable, potentially in our lifetime.

CHAPTER 10: KIDS AND BLINDFOLDED SIGHT

Children develop these abilities much quicker than adults. This partly is due to the lack of ego in a child. They are simply discovering everything for the first time. They are closer to being pure spirit. As we age, we become engrossed in the material and we lose that childlike spark and innocent joy that we used to have. Children between the ages of 6-12 they are running around in delta and theta brainwaves which is a direct opening into their subconscious, which is programming their minds constantly, and uploading all information. Another reason that children may have it easier, aside from brainwaves and subconscious beliefs, is the potential calcification of our pineal gland as we age. Not only that, but we produce less melatonin when we get older too. Decalcifying the pineal gland is a thing, but I will not be covering it in this book. There are several methods and other wonderful resources widely available.

These are Muscles, not Gifts

Many people believe that these psychic skills are gifts, and in a sense, they are but also they are not. Everyone can achieve these things, these abilities are muscles and not gifts. You were born conscious which means you are capable of working with spirit because that's what you are.

Magic is Real

In Indonesia, the Royal family of central Java is capable of extraordinary things. The children are taught at a very young age the interconnectedness of matter and spirit, and how to manipulate them. The children are shown that these things are possible by having family members floating into the room when the child is young. When the children get older they too are levitating objects back and forth and even controlling small remote control cars with their energy. This is how the future could be for all of us. We are truly capable of magical things. It's up to us to make this a reality for the world.

Intensive breathwork is not recommended for young children. They do not need to do the Wim Hof breathing method. If you truly want to start off right, teaching meditation can be very powerful for the child's spiritual development. Children tend to astral project and not even realize they were doing it. This can train children young when these abilities come to use more easily.

Get a Mindfold Mask

Blindfolded sight and the development of your sixth sense has been shown to help children with learning problems and even social anxiety, giving them confidence in themselves. By developing these skills you also find increases in IQ, memory, and overall mental function. You will need a good blindfold to start. Anything to cover your eyes. In some schools, they even tape over the student's eyes to keep them shut. I recommend getting a Mindfold mask for your training.

The Blind vs. the Sighted

When working with children, there is a distinction made between those who can see and those who have been blind since birth. The children who can see already have a mental framework of the world and are generally able to develop their blind-

folded sight more quickly. Children who are blind from birth, on the other hand, have never actually seen anything and they have much less of an idea of what things should even look like. They lack a basic framework that other students already start with. For example, a completely blind child has never seen colors before and has no idea what they should even look like. This can present challenges but they can be overcome. If it is a blind adult you are working with, it may be better to start with energy training and environment detection first. (Covered in the next chapter.)

Practice Makes Perfect

When teaching completely blind children you would want to start with just white and black pieces of paper until the student can tell you 100% of the time whether he has the black page or the white one. This is helping the child develop their intuition as they struggle to truly see. I would recommend still using a blindfold when training with completely blind children. We don't want any light telling the brain to create serotonin instead of melatonin.

Some other practices that you can perform with your child would be to move furniture around the house and have them navigate the new terrain. You can have them follow you around and try and copy the same things that you are doing. We do want to develop sight but we are also training our intuition as well so simple games like guessing heads or tales can be very effective with practice. Pin the tail on the donkey is another fun and effective training method for developing blindfolded sight. Do games all the time like, guess how many fingers I have up behind my back or, which card am I holding.

We need to learn to develop a sense of what our intuition is saying as opposed to our imagination. This really only comes with time and practice. The development of these abilities greatly coincides with the amount of time that you are willing to put into learning and practicing them. Daily meditation and practice discerning colors is very valuable. These skills can come quickly or take a very long time depending on our own effort and attitude.

If You're Having Trouble

If the children are having trouble after practice with colors, you can incorporate slow breathing and begin energy-sensing with the palms. When we gather information and learn to see without our eyes we are tapping into the fields of chi, which are based outside time and space, and encompass everything in a single point. Learning to sense this energy physically, as well as mentally, using intention, we can help our whole system improve. Progress can be helped in all areas when the person has begun energy development in conjunction with their consciousness and intuition training. These things all go hand in hand and help each other out. When kids are learning blindfolded sight as well they tend to see clearer sooner than adults and this should be their main focus until they can begin practicing long-range sight and even looking into the past.

The Subconscious

For a beginners class, the first objective would be to convince the minds of the students that this is all possible and that they too can achieve these things. The biggest obstacle, after all, is going to be ourselves. When there is a battle between the subconscious mind and the conscious mind the subconscious always wins. Once the students understand that this is indeed very real, maybe by sensing subtle energy themselves, then they have made the first step to achieving blindfolded sight. One way you can describe blindfolded sight is by relating it to wifi. Wifi is everywhere, it's just invisible waves emanating through the house that are deciphered into information by your phone or computer. In this same way, our brains decode the radiation emanating off of all objects to sense them in space.

In the next chapter, I will talk about specific methods of training the body to improve your energy sensing, storage, and manipulation capabilities. But for now, we will focus on several other training and practice methods that are well suited for kids. The first step guessing and developing a sense of colors. Give the child

a blue piece of paper and a yellow piece of paper. Tell them which ones they have in which hands and tell them to really try and see them. Get a sense of what those colors are. Then, with practice they will improve their sense of which paper they have. You can now introduce red and green and practice with these 4 colors until they achieve a 100% accuracy rating. Then you can add multiple objects and depth. Colors can be sensed in more ways than just seeing. Each color has a different feel and frequency to it. This information can be gathered not only directly into our brains but also through our nervous system and the feel of an objects energy. We are electric beings after all. For trouble seeing meditate and focus and intend on seeing light. For beginners it can start as a pinhole or a few pinholes in the mask, then with time it develops and fills out more and more of your vision. Blindfolded sight can also start in several different ways for different people. It can start as a flash of light or a smokey haze. It can be a line or a pinhole of light you grow bigger with your concentration to look through. Or it can just be gray fuzz on a black background.

Move Around

After colors, you can try and develop your sense of spatial awareness. This may come naturally for the children, as they find ways to play and keep the mood joyful rather than serious. This is also another important factor to consider when teaching, or trying to learn blindfolded sight. Your mood is very important and can have a large impact on your success. When we keep things playful we tend to learn much faster than when we are very serious with punishment involved. This activates different parts of the brain and can cause it to fire incoherently. When we are happy and in a good mood our brain works better and fires with coherence. Keeping people calm will bring the brain into a natural state of coherence. Stress and anger, on the other hand, will shut off parts of the brain from communicating which is followed by narrow-mindedness and a temporary drop in reasoning and IQ.

Be Happy

Keep the mood playful, happy and simple. Guessing colors then following you around and avoiding obstacles. Maybe picking up the right color of paper off of the ground or guessing which way the arrow is pointing. Once sight begins to come in you can begin playing with reading letters blindfolded. Some advice for this, is in the early stages, make sure you put the student's finger on the letter and that it is large enough for them to trace and feel on the paper. Not and change in elevation or thick ink but rather feel the energy of the colors and where the edges of one end and the next begins. With dedication, reading can come on the third day or sooner. This also brings the possibility for other fun games like separating cards or reading a book. You can even try games like, "what do I have in this box?", or "what item was on this table 1 minute ago?"

CHAPTER 11: ADULTS AND TRAINING BLINDFOLDED SIGHT

Adults

Adults are generally more difficult to train. Don't be discouraged though, we are all capable of learning these things. For adults, the road only becomes more complex and full of understanding. For us, we often have to understand something for our analytical mind to accept it and allow it to work toward achieving that goal. Adults run into more mental roadblocks than children because of their egos getting in the way. So for adults, the first step may be reading this whole book, rather than just jumping into the water without knowing if it's real. You want to slowly work with the subconscious to build the foundation for these abilities to arise. Another important step, is to have a good blindfold. I recommend the Mindfold mask over any other as it works the best, completely shutting out the lights, and allowing you to open your eyes while the mask is on.

Meditation

Meditation for an hour a day is highly recommended for the beginner who wants to learn any of the supernatural abilities that are demonstrated by high-level yogis and enlightened masters.

We need meditation so we can learn to change brainwave frequencies as well as produce DMT on demand. Guided meditations and hypnosis, or suggestions made when the subject is in the theta state can be very effective in removing mental blocks and fears which inhibit progress. Some great guided meditation materials are Robert Monroes, Gateway Program, as well as several audiobooks by Jose Silva.

Yogic Breathing

Next Yogic breathing is very important in training and developing the right physiology in the body to help these things occur. Remember we are our spirit constantly unfolding in manifestation. We need to bring our bodies into a healthy and happy state to allow harmonious action. Wim hof breathing is a great breath technique to jump into the deep end and effect the right changes we are looking for. Later in your practice, this may not be needed as much and you will focus more on the breath retention and movement techniques developed in Merpati Putih.

The Wim Hof Breathing technique: (To be done sitting or laying down)

30 Large breaths in continuous succession. (about 1-2 seconds each)

On the last breath, exhale completely and hold for a minute and a half.

Then, Inhale and press the air into your head. (You may get some DMT)

Repeat five or more times.

Do before training

(See the Breathwork chapter for benefits)

Seeing the Light

A great beginner technique is to use the Mindfold Mask in a dark room with a flashlight. Make sure beforehand that there are no holes or gaps visible in the mask. You then begin by doing breathwork for 10 minutes. You breathe in for 8 seconds, hold for 8 seconds, breath out for 8 seconds, and hold for 8 seconds. This is

called square breathing and it can help your mind and body come into the right state for these subtle senses. After 10 minutes of this breathing, continue the breathwork while also bringing the flashlight up to the mask to look for the light. Pull it away and bring it back. Move your head around and look for a light. Try shining it on the back of your head. Some people develop a point of perception on the back of their head first. You may notice this by turning the light on and off or moving your hand in front of it. Play with it and do this for several days in a row until you get results. Add it into your daily practice routine.

Work Out

Stretching is also important for ensuring that you have proper blood and chi flow throughout the system. Exercising the body also helps the mind. This whole training encompasses body, mind, and spiritual elements. It's highly recommended to work out for at least 30 minutes before doing your energy movements as this will allows for the greatest effects. Energy development can be slow at first but with time it will increase. Your first step is spending about three months training your body, mind, and spirit with these breathing and energy movements.

The Merpati Putih Movements (To be performed blindfolded)

First, sit with your right leg over your left, and bring your hands together in a prayer posture in front of the middle of your chest, or your solar plexus. With your thumbs touching your chest, you will exhale, while leaning forward and pointing the tips of your fingers down to the ground. With pursed lips, the exhaling sound will be "shhh." When you reach the bottom of your bow you will pop back up at twice the speed you bent forward with, returning to the original starting position, and inhaling swiftly through the nose. Now with your hand back in prayer posture, you will press them firmly together keeping the tension in your arms and shoulders. You will move your hands slowly forward away from your chest until they are pointed directly away from you with

your thumbs touching and fingers together and pointed up. Next, while keeping tension in your arms you will extend them horizontally out into a human cross or an eagle spreading its wings. Then, keeping your arms level and not lopsided, you will bring them forward back pressing out in front of you as if you have pushed something away. Your fingertips remaining facing the sky the whole time with tension pulling back to your shoulders, bring your palms back together and straight back to your chest. Firmly put pressure on your hands pressing together, then bow forward and exhale, finally popping back up for a small breather. Your hands can rest on your knees palms facing up. This whole movement and the following movements will follow a similar breathing pattern. Exhale, breath in, and hold your breath as long as you can while you slowly and smoothly execute your movements with maximum tension in your arms.

Our second energy movement begins sitting in the same position but with our arms up above our heads palms facing forward. We then lean forward in our bow, exhaling at the same time with pursed lips, making the "shh" sound. Our arms stay straight and move down to the ground in front of us splitting away and moving to our sides as if pushing through the water in a breast stroke. once our head is at its lowest point, without touching the ground, and our arms are behind us, palms up, we reverse the motion and inhale bringing our spine and arms back straight up with our hands above our head. Now we will hold our breath and slowly clench our fists while we bring our hands down in straight lines to our waist with our elbows pointing behind us. We will have tension in our arms and fists throughout this breath-hold. with your fists closed tight at your waist sides, palms facing up, you will punch both arms out in front of you, fists rotating 180-degrees to palms down, straight out as far as you can. Then, pull your fists back to your sides at your hips, hands closed, palms up. You will do this punching movement again going forward to extension and returning to bent arms at the hips. Then on a third and final punch forward with your arms straight out in front of

you, thumbs close together, you will open your fists to flat hands, facing forward, fingers up. Then with your exhale you will bow down again and move your arms out to the sides ending behind you, where you can breathe in lean back up to a straight sitting position. You may breath normally for a moment, bringing your hands back to their resting position on your knees with your palms open and facing up.

Our third energy movement is like a mixture of the two previous movements. You begin with your arms up above your head, with your palms facing forward. You then exhale with pursed lips making the "shh" sound as you bow forward. Your arms stay parallel and straight in this movement and they come all the way down to the floor making contact palms down in a bow. You can also touch your head to the ground if you are flexible enough. You then come back up inhaling through the nose, bringing your arms all the way straight above your head to their starting position. You will then slowly bring your hands straight down, grabbing the life energy above you and clenching your fists pulling it into your body. Your hands will pull down moving in a straight line ending at your waist with your elbows behind you and your hands facing up in fists. You will then do a punching motion forward, like the previous movement, except once your arms are straight out in front of you, you open your fists with your fingers to the sky, flexing, pulling toward your shoulders. You will then move them to your sides in a horizontal motion keeping them level ending in the cross position. Once they are fully extended out like an eagle you will bring your hands down and around to your hips, hands flat and finger-pointing forward to a pushing motion, where your arms return straight out in front of you with your hands open and your fingers to the sky. You then clench your fist grabbing more energy and pulling it into your center. You do one more punch from the hips, and on your final extension your hands open up and you exhale bowing and pushing the energy to the sides and back ending with your arms behind you and your palms facing up. Then you can inhale, straighten back up, and

place your hands on your knees for another small breather.

The fourth energy movement begins with your arms above your head once again, with your palms facing forward. You do a pursed-lip exhale while bowing forward. Your arms remain straight all the way to the floor. With your inhale you raise them once again to the starting position and you hold your breath. Your palms remade facing forward as you close your first and bend them at a 90-degree angle at the wrist. Your elbows bend as your hands drop in a straight line down to the level of your forehead (imagine a praying mantis). Your arms then cross with your right arm over your left arm and you squeeze with maximum tension. You bow and bring your crossed arms above your head shaking with tension. When you need to breathe you then straighten your back, bring your fists into our familiar position at the waist, and we do one punch forward, opening our hands, fingers to the sky, then exhaling on a bow forward pushing our arms to our sides and behind us. We may then breathe normally straightening up, and resting our hands on our knees, with our palms facing up.

Standing Movements

These energy building movements can be done when we are standing as well as when we are sitting. When we are standing and we do these movements, we want to make sure we have a good base, with our legs slightly bent. When we do our initial bows for the second, third, and fourth movements our hands will come all the way down between our legs and behind our ankles. This is where your inhale for each movement begins bringing your head back up to its starting position and raising your arms drawing in vital energy. When we finally exhale after holding our breath in the standing exercises, you just push the energy out and to your sides, you don't need to bend down to your ankles again. Only when we are standing, and at the beginning of the second, third, and fourth movements, not the end.

I Have Online Classes

There are several more movements not mentioned. I go over all

those listed above, and a couple more in my blindfolded sight online workshop. I was able to acquire them, without having to sign an NDA from MP-USA, because the Indonesian government put them temporarily on youtube to help their people battle Covid-19. In Indonesia, the survival rate is close to 95%. Here in the US, we have many high-quality hospitals and ventilators handy, so our survival rate is over 99%, but other countries were not as readily equipped as us. So instead they introduced breathing and energy generation techniques because of their proven effectiveness at helping fight Covid-19, strengthening the lungs and improving the body's overall vitality and resilience.

You will want to do these every day. These energy movements can leave you feeling charged so it's recommended that you do double sets and avoid practice right before bed, as it can make it hard to sleep, unless you're aiming to dive deep and try meditating instead of sleeping like the monks training in Himalayan caves.

Square Breathing

These movements should be followed by slow breathing extending from 4 seconds in 4 seconds out to longer and longer breaths with holds placed in between. Then you will work on energy sensing using your hands and developing your senses. The slow breathing will push more oxygen into the system allowing it to optimize as well as increase your energy-sensing abilities. Not only should you practice feeling and increasing the density of your field but feeling the sensations of energy all over your body, not just in your hands. You will learn to ball energy up and distribute it anywhere you would like for a variety of uses. This energy is programmable with our intention and can be expressed in a variety of ways. We can take this energy and use it for healing or environmental detection. This is the energy that people use when they do reiki healings and energy healing in Chinese hospitals. There are videos of a woman's large tumor shrinking and disappearing after just 2.5 minutes using energy healing.

Tension is Key

When you do your energy movements with greater tension and flexing you will feel stronger sensations of chi. After the movements, you will breathe slowly and feel the sensations between your hands holding them six inches apart. You will pulse your hands in and out and feel the magnetic force, the push and pull. It's also recognized as a warm buzzing. One good way to create this sensation without the movements is to put your fingernails together and rub them back and forth for 30 seconds. After this, you will feel the warm buzzing and the slight magnetism of your hands. Play with changing the polarity from push to pull. Notice that when you move your focussed attention across your hand it is like dragging a finger across your hand. Where your attention goes your energy flows. Bring your hands up to your face, a few inches away, and see if you can sense the energy on your cheeks or forehead. The more your practice sensing this energy the better and more refined your senses will become. Following energy-sensing, you would finish off with a meditation focusing on compassion. You can feel your heart chakras electromagnetic field emanating from your chest. Bring energy into this field by bringing your hands to your chest and breathing through your heart. Feel resounding love for yourself and all things. This increases your electromagnetic field strength and your brain coherence. After this meditation, from anywhere between 5 minutes to 1 hour, you will begin your color recognition and your environment detection. It's best to do these exercises with a partner who can give you biofeedback without you having to lift up your mask.

Energy Exercises with a Friend

Some other energy exercises to do with a friend are to have one person blindfolded while the other person holds up their hand in a "high five" position. The blindfolded person will now put up their hand in front of them maybe 6-10 inches away, and they will scan their hand up, down, and sided to side as if dragging it on a

flat wall in front of them until they sense the other person's hand and feel confident moving it forward for a high five. The blindfolded person will then find out how accurate they were and if they could sense the other person's energy well enough. Sensing energy is easier when you are calm and in a relaxed state. More of these exercises can be performed when each person has developed adequate energy-sensing abilities not only in their hand but over their whole body. They can then feel when someone is approaching behind them and exactly how far away they are. You can also form this image in your mind and see behind you directing your field of view from the front to the back while blindfolded.

Moving Perception

You will find that when developing your extrasensory capabilities, you can move your perception to anywhere in the room, as well as anywhere in existence. You can even do things like creating a split-screen, of sorts, and view either two objects side by side, or two views of the same object side by side. One good practice for this is to try and see your arms when blindfolded. These are often the first things you will see moving around in the dark. Take one of your hands and put it behind your back. Then try and see your hand as if it is right in front of your face. Explore and play with this especially at night once you have laid down for a while and area near sleep. As your brainwaves drop seeing the subtle energies become much easier. Try and look around your room with your eyes closed in the dark, and try and see where the window is and the corners of the room. Look for the various furniture. Get up and walk around while you have some depth perception. One thing to note when you first begin developing this field vision, depth perception can be a little off due to your ability to shift your perspective.

Astral Projection

One more thing that helps with the development of blindfolded

sight is astral projection. When you roll out of your body you can see your room in astral form even though your eyes are closed. This is the same concept and stems from your ability to decipher energy into information. Improving one ability often improves others. I will give you a quick lesson on astral projection. First, you want to lay on your back and stay conscious until your body falls asleep and enters a state of sleep paralysis. Play rem frequencies while so you can enter and extend your trip. Also, self-hypnosis and affirmations that you will, indeed, remember everything from your astral travels. While you lay there waiting, imagine that you are in your room standing up. In your mind do everything that you can to make it seem as real as possible, smell, touch, and move things. Jump and listen. Examine an object, or feel your own skin. This will help prepare you for what you are attempting to do. This is important as normally our brains breakdown dreams incredibly fast. But we can train ourselves to remember. Around the time that your body will be falling asleep, you may enter into a very loud and turbulent white tunnel. Do not be alarmed it can actually get pretty loud. Once you pass through this tunnel and find your body fast asleep do not panic when you cannot move because of sleep paralysis. You're not being abducted, you haven't been drugged, you're getting ready to astral travel. You must just wait a little longer being relaxed and then tell yourself you're going to roll out of your body in 3... 2...1 and roll as if you are physically moving your actual body, but because it is in sleep paralysis, you will move your astral body instead and roll out of the darkness of your skull and into the sight of your room. Ta-da! You've just astral projected! Now explore and have fun!

Answers From the Ether

Next just like the progression of the children you start with colors and training your intuition. With adults, they find that most of the information will come in a question and answer form. For example, when trying to see they may instead ask, "what is in front of me?" And they get the answer, "a banana."

With practice on developing DMT with breathing techniques and meditation, you will be able to see as well. Just like the children, it can greatly help to have a smile on your face when you are trying to learn, and also to practice in the sunlight when you have the chance, as the brighter it is, the more vibrant the energy. You can also develop the ability to see in the dark. The Indonesian special forces have done this in place of night vision technology. They are called, the Kopassus.

Timeline

Practice makes perfect. If you'd like an idea on how long it can take to learn these skills you can look at several of the workshops that are put together. When you spend thousands to go to a workshop somewhere around the world they will spend 4-5 hours a day for 5 days to train you. So that's putting in the time of a part-time job to get good results. Most people have a hard time dedicating even a fraction of this time to training and they see only a fraction of the results. Breathing, energy movements, meditation, and real-world practice is how you achieve blindfolded sight.

Get a Group

I would highly recommend getting a group of like-minded people who can train with you and practice sensing energy blindfolded. Having someone to hand you different colors of paper, or move objects around for you to reach for, on your first try, is very helpful. I do have a program in my workshop on my website, blindfoldedsight.com that is very helpful for the solo learner. Treat this like a game and make it fun. The less stress the better. Meditating will help this and also bring you into the right state of mind. It's found that a majority of psychic phenomena, when tested in a lab, happened around 7.83 Hz, or the Schumann resonance. This is when we are in the theta brainwave state, when we can generate DMT production and begin to form vivid images in our mind. Practicing meditation with binaural beats utilizing this frequency can be greatly beneficial.

Be Right Brained

When we are training these things we are working with the right and the left side of the brain. The right side is the analytical, logical side which dominates most of humanity. And the left side is the imagination, feeling, and spiritual side of the brain. We primarily want to work on the right side of the brain. One way to do this is to distract the left side of the brain by tapping your head or plugging your nose. This allows the right side of the brain to temporarily peak through. This method is one of distraction, but primarily we want to aim for a biofeedback approach to learning. If we can have the brain in synchronization, preferably without binaural beats in the long run, but they are effective early on. Biofeedback is when the right and left sides of the brain work together rather than suppressing one side of the brain over the other. This is why it takes time to learn and develop these skills. Anyone can have an intuitive hot streak but to actually develop and train these skills we have to go through the trials to learn ourselves what is right and what is wrong.

Don't Think

Another important aspect of this training is being able to move past your imagination. Often if we are distracted the answer will just come right to us. When we have a clear mind it's easier to detect the subtle answer. One good way to practice with this is to go with the first answer that popped into your head. You don't want to guess over and over, you want to know. Questioning yourself can be detrimental, so just go with your instinct and you will learn slowly when it's saying something and when you're making it up. Go with the flow, don't guess, know.

Your training goes like this:

The first 3 months
Wim Hof Breath
Work Out
Energy Movements
Energy Sensing

Coherence Meditation
Color recognition
Environment Detection

Put in the training, if you skip a couple of days in the beginning, your accuracy ratings may drop back down if they have risen. Every step counts. These skills are just the beginning of incredible feats and epic journeys into the future.

CONCLUSION

Be the Change

We have now reached the end of book 1. I plan on writing more as I learn more. Look out for books regarding advanced techniques in blindfolded sight, telepathy, telekinesis, pyrokinesis, and even levitation. This book has been a fundamental intro to the basics. Each ability is different and comes with its own set of skills to master. Starting with your intuition is one of the best ways to further your development down all of the different secret teachings of siddhis, or superpowers.

These abilities often stem from forming and maintaining a connection. Remember, to connect to source, you must:
Understand the perfection in all things
Treat everyone as if they are you
Love everyone unconditionally

Also, you must remember the fundamental fabric that you work with.
All points in space and time are one
Everything is energy
Consciousness is the bases for all

If you have picked up and read through this book then there is a spark in you. You can feel it inside. I hope I only fanned the flame and helped it grow. You can achieve the impossible.

"Whatever the mind can conceive and believe, it can achieve."

—**Napoleon Hill**

I will leave you with words of Jesus from The Life and Teachings of the Masters of the Far East.

Jesus said, " When we stand one with the sum of all intelligence and recognize ourselves as an actual part of that intelligence, and know conclusively that this is the great principle, god, we shall soon find ourselves conscious of the fact that all intelligence throughout the cosmic universe is working with us. we also realize quickly that the intelligence of all great genius, as well as the little mentality of a single cell of the body, is working with us in perfect harmony and accord. This is the one great intelligence of cosmic mind that we are positively allied with, indeed we are that allied mind. We are the self-consciousness of that cosmic universe. The instant we feel this very thing, nothing can keep us from the godhead. From the universal consciousness, we can draw all knowledge. We know that we can know all without studying and without process of reasoning. Not going from one lesson to another, nor from one point to another. The lessons are only necessary in order to bring us to the attitude in which we can step forth into this thought. Then we become comprehensive and include all thoughts. There is a complete stream of thought that is irresistible, and we know that nothing can divert us from true accomplishment. We are with the whole, thus we move on irresistibly with the whole. It is impossible for any condition to keep us from our accomplishment.
The drop of water is only weak when it is removed from the ocean. Replace it, and it is as powerful as the whole ocean. It matters not whether we like it or whether we believe it. It is intelligent law, and we are that very thing. The sum of all truth is the great principle, God. Everything from eternity to eternity, whether we think it a great truth or a little truth. Every truth, thought, or word, spoken, is a part of the great truth. One great all. One universal truth, and we are that very thing. When we realize this oneness, and stand absolutely with truth, we have the whole of the truth back of us and our irresistibility is increased. It is the

force of the ocean back of the wave that gives the wave its power. That too is but a portion of God's force, which man also is. The sum of all love is the great principle, God. It is the sum of every affection. Every fervent emotion. Every loving thought, look, word, or deed. Every attracted love, great or small, sublime or low, makes the one infinite love stand forth, and nothing is too great for us. As we love unselfishly we have the complete ocean of cosmic love with us. That which is thought least is greatest as it sweeps on to absolute perfection. Thus the whole universe of love is consciously with us. There is no greater power on earth or in heaven than pure love. Earth becomes heaven. Humanities true home.

Finally the sum of every condition, every form, every being is the one infinite cosmic principle God. Whether it be individual, worlds, planets, stars, atoms, electrons, or the most minute particles. All together make one infinite whole. The body of which is the universe. The mind is cosmic intelligence. The soul, cosmic love, molded together as a whole. Their bodies are held together by a cohesive force of love, yet each one functions in eternal, individual identity. Moving freely in its own individual orbit and octave or harmony, attracted, drawn, and held together by that universe of harmony. We constitute that being, that nothing can thwart. It is made up of every unit of humanity as well as every unit of the universe. If a portion of one unit excludes itself from the whole, it makes no difference to principle being, but it makes a vast difference to the unit. The ocean is not conscious of the removal of the drop of water, but the drop is very conscious of the ocean when it is returned or reunited. It is not enough to say that we are close to the great cosmic principle God, we must know that we are one, in, and of, entirely amalgamated with principle. Thus we work with principle of power which is all power. It is the law, that in principle, we live, move, and have our being. Thus when we wish to come in contact with God, we do not think of something far away from us and difficult to attain. All we need know is that God is within as well as all about us, and that we are completely included in God. That we are present with God and in

command with full power. Thus we need not pause, we need not ponder. We take the path directly to God within. Here, the Christ stands steadfast and supreme and with God, we endure forever. Thus we arouse our dead cells to the realization of the life within, and that life resurrects us from the dead. We return to life immortal, unchanging. We are condensed of life, or of our right to live that life fully and perfectly. The Christ within stands forth and says, I come that you may have complete life and live that life more abundantly. This must be a true resurrection in our consciousness, an uplifting of our dead senes into a higher vibration of life, truth, and love. As all nature is awakening about us, let us see the dawn of the approaching day. Thus we get up and out of our grave clothes. Up and out of our sense of limitation, in which we have bound our bodies. We roll the stone of materiality completely from our consciousness, that heavy weight of thought that has separated the life within, from the life without. And which has held the life form in death as we have not recognized its right to life. Let us get up and out of death, that is what the resurrection means. It is an awakening to the full realization of life here and now. And that life, omniscient, omnipresent, omnipotent, nowhere absent, nowhere powerless, nowhere unconscious, but everywhere present, everywhere powerful, everywhere conscious, in fullness, in freedom, in glorious radiant expressive expanding action. When our hearts flame to this thought and our whole being glows with this light within, we can readily extend our hand and say, "Lazarus come forth. Get out of your grave, you do not belong in death. Come to life. Awake from your delusion. Awake now and here." Thus we are awakened to the master's conscious and we shall weep because of the density of thoughts of those who watch the awakening. Thousands of years of this awakening have been presented to humanity, yet many sleep. But their sleeping does not justify us in doing so. It is because of what we do that humanity is awakened to that rightful heritage. As we awaken to our heritage, we shall awaken to the purity of that age-old message, that our bodies are eternally beautiful, pure, and perfect. They are always beautiful, pure, spiritual bodies, most

magnificent and divine. The true temples of God. This awakening also convinces us that our bodies have never descended from the highest state. We see that it was only in a human concept, wherein we thought they had descended. As soon as this thought is released, our body is released to its true inheritance of divinity. Then a fragrance of a warm summer evening suffices all nature, and our bodies begin to take on the effulgence. Soon pure rays of white light appear within our bodies, they become aglow with this light, and this soft yet brilliant living light invades the clear atmosphere around us like a white gold vapor. This light increases steadily until it covers and permeates everything about it. Bathed in this radiance there appears a crystal white light, dazzling and scintillating, with a radiance greater than that of the purest diamond. Yet it is emanating from our bodies, and they stand forth ablaze with pure light, radiant and beautiful. Here we stand together on the holy mount of transfiguration, with bodies luminous and glowing, radiant and beautiful. Emerged wholly in divine light. The son of man has become the Christ of God, and the kingdom of God is once more among mankind. And more vital because others have accepted and brought forth in full dominion. The light of the God kingdom grows stronger because of the acceptance. This is a new age message to you. The same as it seemed to be a new message 2,000 years ago. It is the same today as it was then. It is but a resurrection of the age-old message. This message was told thousands of centuries ago in language so simple that babes could read. The message is that man, of his own free will, shall leave the manmade kingdom and evolve to the God kingdom. The son of man is to realize his divinity, reveal this divinity in his body and affairs, and become the Christ of God, in the kingdom of God. Know ye not that ye are Gods? Within you, know that the kingdom of God is the most natural thing in the world. You have but overlooked the fact that if man be in Christ, he is a new creature. It is the father's good pleasure to give you the kingdom, and every man passes into it. The question is asked, when? The answer always is, when the without is as the within.

The great oak tree that sleeps within the acren, became aroused

throughout the whole acren, before the tree could develop. I have not seen nor ear heard, nor have been entered into the heart of man to conceive of the things that God has prepared for them that love him. God knows that in the structure of the universe there is a splendid place for every human being and that each has his individual place. The structure can stand only because each is in his right place. Does not the message lighten the burden of everyone and adorn each countenance with a smile? Even those of the weary ones who think they labor like dumb driven cattle. Thus, I say to you, that you are a specially designed creation. You have a particular mission. You have a light to give and work to do that no other can give or accomplish. And if you will open your heart mind and soul wide to spirit, you will learn of it in your own heart. There you find that your very own father speaks to you. No matter how wayward or thoughtless you thought yourself. You will find that your father loves you devotedly, and tenderly, the instant you turn to God within. The anointing which you have of God, abides in you, and you need not the teachings of any man. Is this not a resurrection from thought. You need not that any man teaches you, it is only necessary to receive the anointing from God, that has always been yours. You may accept others as brother helpers, but you are always instructed and lead from within. The truth is there for you, and you will find it. That truth always teaches that humanity is a complete unit, not a unity, but a great unit. Combined with God, they are the great one. Humanity is more than a brotherhood, it is one man, just as a vine and its branches are one vine. No one part or one unit can be separated from the whole. The Christ prayer is that they all may be one. He that has done it unto the least of my brethren has done it unto me. Now you know the Christ for whom the whole family in heaven and on earth is named. The truth is, all is one, one spirit, one body. The great lord body of all humanity, the great love and life of God completely amalgamated that body into one complete whole. You can see and talk with God at any time. Just as you can with father, mother, brother or sister. Indeed, he is far closer than any mortal could be. God is far dearer and truer than any friend. God is

never wrought up or angry or cast down. God never destroys or hinders or hurts any of his creatures or creations. If God did these things, he would not be God. The God that judges destroys, or withholds any good thing from his children or creatures or creations is but a god that is conjured up by man's ignorant thinking, and you need not fear that God unless you wish to do so. For the true God stretches forth his hand and says, " All that I have is yours." When one of your poets said, "God is closer than breathing and nearer than hands or feat." He was inspired by God. All are inspired by God when that inspiration is for the good or the right. And all can be inspired by God at all times if they only willed. When I said I am the Christ the only begotten of God. I did not declare this for myself alone, for had I done this, I could not have become the Christ. I say definitely that, in order to bring forth the Christ I and all others must declare it, then must live the life, and the Christ must appear. You may declare the Christ all you will, but if you do not live the life the Christ will not appear. Just think dear friends, if all would declare the Christ and live the life for one year or five years, what an awakening there would be. The possibilities cannot be imagined. That was the vision that I saw, dear ones, can you not place yourselves where I stood? See as I saw? Why do you surround me with the murk and the mire of superstition? Why do you not lift your minds and eyes and thoughts above these, and see with a clearer vision? Then, you would see that there are no miracles, no mysteries, no pain, no imperfection, no inharmony, no death, except that which man has made. When I said, "I have overcome death," I knew from where I spoke, but it took crucifixion to show these dear ones. There is a great many of us joined together to help the whole world, and this is our life work. There have been times when it has taken our combined energy to ward off the evil thoughts of doubt and disbelief and superstition that have nearly engulfed mankind. You may call them evil forces if you wish. We know that they are only evil as man makes them so. And now we see the light growing brighter and brighter as the dear ones throw off the bonds. The throwing off of these bonds may for a time sink mankind into materiality,

but even so, it is a step nearer the goal. For materiality does not hold one as superstition and myth and mystery hold one. When I stepped on the water that day, do you think that I cast my eyes downward into the great depths, the material substance? No, I fastened my eyes steadfastly on God power that transcends any power of the deep. The moment I did this, the water became as firm as a rock, and I could walk upon it with perfect safety."

One man in the party asks Jesus, " Can all bring forth the Christ?" Jesus responds, "Yes there is but one end of accomplishment, man came forth from God and he must return to god. That which from the heavens descended must again ascend into the heavens. The history of the Christ did not begin with my birth. Neither did it end with the crucifixion. The Christ was created when God created the first man in his own image and likeness. The Christ and that man are one. All men and that man are one. As God was the father, so is he, the father of all men, and all are God's children. As the child has the quality of the parent, so the Christ is in every child. For many years the child lived and realized his Christ-hood, his oneness with God, through the Christ in himself. Then began the history of the Christ, and you can trace this history back to man's beginning. That the Christ means more than the man Jesus goes without contradiction. Had I not perceived this I could not have brought forth the Christ, to me this is the pearl without price, the old wine in new bottles. The truth which many others have brought forth and thus have fulfilled the ideal that I have fulfilled and proved. For more than 50 years after that day upon the cross, I taught and lived with my disciples, and many of those I love dearly. Those days we gathered at a quiet place just outside of Judea. There we were free of the prying eyes of superstition. Their many acquired the great gifts and they accomplished great work. Then seeing by withdrawing for a time, I would be able to reach and help all, I withdrew. Besides, they were depending upon me instead of depending upon themselves, and in order for them to be self-reliant, it was important for me to withdraw from them. If they lived in close association with me, then could they not find me again if they desired to do so. The cross, in the begin-

ning, was the symbol for the greatest joy the world ever knew. The foundation of the cross is the place where man first trod the earth. Therefore, the mark that symbolizes the dawn of the celestial day here on earth. If you will trace it back, you will find that the cross disappears entirely and that it is the man, standing in the attitude of devotion. Standing in space with arms upraised in blessing, sending out his gifts to humanity, pouring all his gifts forth freely in every direction. When you know that the Christ is the fitting life within the form. The raising energy that the scientists glimpse yet not know whence it came. When you feel with the Christ, that the life is lived so that life may be given freely. When you learn that man is obliged to live with the constant dissolution of form, and that the Christ lived to give up the thing that the body sense craved, for the good that at the moment you could not yet enjoy. You are the Christ. When you see yourself a part of the greater, willing to sacrifice for the whole. When you learn to do the right without being affected by the outcome to help. When you learn freely to give up physical life and all that the world has to give. this is not self abdication or poverty. For as you give of God you will find you have more to give. Although at times duty may seem to demand all that life has to give. You will also know that he who will save his life, shall lose it. Then you will see that the purest gold is at the deepest part of the furnace, where the fire has fully cleansed it. You will find great joy in knowing that the life you have given to others is the life you have won. You will know that to receive, is to give freely. That if you lay down the mortal form, a higher life will prevail. You have the glad assurance that a life thus won is won for all. You must know that the great Christ soul can go down to the river, and stepping into the water but tiplifies the sympathy you feel for the world's great need. Then you are able to help your fellow man and not boast of virtue. You can pass out the bread of life to the hungry souls that come to you, yet that bread never diminishes by the giving. You must press on and know fully that you are able to heal all that comes to you, sick, or weary, or heavy laden with the word that makes whole the soul. You are able to open the eyes of those made

blinded either by ignorance or choice. It does not matter how low the blindfold may be. He must feel that the Christ soul stands inside him and you must find that with human feet you tread the very ground that he treads. Then you will know that the true unity of father and son is within and not without. You will know that you must stand serene when the God without is put away, and only the God within remains. You must be able to withhold a cry of love and fear, as the words, "My god my god why have you forsaken me?" Ring out. Still, at that hour, you must not feel alone, you must know that you stand with God. That you are nearer to the heart of the loving father than you have ever been before. You must know the hour you touch the deepest sorrow is the hour in which your greatest triumph begins. With all this you must know that sorrows cannot touch you. From that hour your voice will ring with a glad free song, for you fully know that you are the Christ. This light, which is to shine among men and for men. Then you will know the darkness in every soul that cannot find a helping hand to clasp as he journeys on the rugged road before he finds the Christ within. You must know that you are truly divine, and being divine you must see that all men are as you are. You will know that there are dark places you must pass with the light that you are to carry to the highest, and your soul will ring out in praise, that you can be of service to all men. Then, with a glad free shout, you mount to your very highest in your union with God. Now you know that there is no substitution for your light, or your life, or other lives, or of your purity for others' sins, but that all are glad free spirits, in and of themselves and of God. You know that you can reach them while they cannot reach each other. That you cannot help giving of your life for the life of each soul, that it shall not perish. Yet you must be so reverent of that soul that you will not pour into it a flood of life, unless the life of that soul opens to receive it. But you will freely pour out to it a flood of love, light and life so that when one does open the windows, the light of God will pour in and illuminate him. You will know that in every Christ that arises, humanity is lifted one step higher. Then too, you must know full well that you have every-

thing that the father has, and having all, it is for all to use. You must know that as you rise and are true, you lift the whole world with you. For as you tread the path it becomes planer for your fellow man. You must have faith in yourself knowing fully. That faith, is God within. Finally, you must know you are a temple of God. A house not made with hand. Immortal in the earth and heaven as well. Then will they sing of you, "All hail all hail, he comes, he comes, the king, and low he is with you always. You are in God and he is in you."

Words spoken by the Enlightened Master Jesus Christ in the 1890's.

Thank you all so much. I truly wish that you continue on your journey of self-realization and self-mastery. Now you have acquired a fantastic fundamental base of knowledge that you can actualize and bring into manifestation. You are an infinite creator with limitless potential. Do not give up, and always chose love over fear. It is better to give than to receive, and unconditional love for all, is the goal we should strive for. Forgiveness is also key, for an eye for an eye, will leave the world blind. Blindfolded-sight.com

By: Robert Smith

Printed in Great Britain
by Amazon

62321285R00058